Bid me discourse, I will enchant thine ear.

– Shakespeare, *Venus and Adonis*

The Enchanted Ear

or

Lured into the Music Box Cosmos

Mostly True Tales Told by
Larry Karp

AN AUTHORS GUILD BACKINPRINT.COM EDITION

Dedicated to

Bill Ullstrom and Joe Ira

The Enchanted Ear
or Lured into the Music Box Cosmos
All Rights Reserved © 1995, 2000 by Larry Karp

AN AUTHORS GUILD BACKINPRINT.COM EDITION

Published by iUniverse.com, Inc.

For information address:
iUniverse.com, Inc.
620 North 48th Street, Suite 201
Lincoln, NE 68504-3467
www.iuniverse.com

Originally published by Emprise Publishing, Inc.

ISBN: 0-595-12129-2

Printed in the United States of America

CRSR

Table of Contents

Henry Rowley Bishop (1786 - 1855), a prolific British composer of musical plays and operas, is best remembered for his immensely popular composition, "Home Sweet Home." But Bishop's fame might more justly be based upon "Bid Me Discourse," a tune he wrote in 1820 for his play, *Twelfth Night*. Listen to this lovely melody as arranged for an 1825 cylinder music box by one of the Swiss master craftsmen of the day. If it doesn't thoroughly enchant your ear, well, you have my deepest sympathy.

Foreword

ot until I was forty-five years old did I realize that there was something special about old music boxes. What's more, a surprising number of my collector-friends tell a similar story. Could be that we're all just a bunch of slow learners. Otherwise, I guess I'm left with the assumption that an expanding waistline can in some mysterious fashion join forces with a receding hairline to raise a person's susceptibility to the voices of mechanical music.

Now, of course it's possible that this association is no more than coincidental — but I don't think that's the case. I think it's for real. I also think that in the last analysis, it has to do with the way we go about the business of living.

We inhabit, each of us, a world largely of our own design, created from the random bits and chunks of material that happen to fall our way. The manner in which we regard this material will in turn determine the manner in which we set our scenes, author our scripts, and act out our plays.

Now, as many of us move along through our worlds, we're dogged by an odd, unsettling notion: the sense that nothing we encounter in our worlds nor anything we do seems terribly important. Our days pass in fidgets, leaving us ever more discontented and dissatisfied. We feel out of kilter –- quite literally, out of place. In worlds we have ourselves put together, we find ourselves strangers. We seem unable to observe the proper customs, and the language remains foreign to our ears and tongues.

Yet, some people do manage to create comfortable worlds for themselves, with very little apparent difficulty, and often from early on in their lives. "I always knew exactly what I wanted to do," my father told me years ago. He spent a half-century teaching literature, grammar, and reading to college students, and after his retirement, he claimed to have no regrets, insisting that given a second life, he would do exactly the same thing with it. Our family doctor spent a similar half-century attending to our illnesses, incapacities, and infirmities with the clear passion of a true lover. Willingly and cheerfully, he placed himself on call for twenty-four hours a day, seven days a week, and nothing less than his own terminal illness ever forced him to miss his rounds or to close the door to his office. As sick as I ever felt, I began to recover the moment Dr. Joelson walked into the room and fixed me with his eye. More than once, I heard one of my elders remark that Doc's ability to diagnose and cure disease was no less than magical.

Why should this be? Why do some people so easily come to recognize what is magical in their surroundings, while others plod –- sometimes their whole lives long –- through endless landscapes of the banal? Is the magic sometimes missing? I don't really think so. I think it's there, all right. But unfortunately, we tend to limit our scope of vision so severely that we simply can not recognize it. We stereotype the manner in which we regard our surroundings, always coming at an object from the same direction, and therefore seeing only a very small part of it. Even worse, we may wilfully put aside as inappropriate or inconsequential something which may happen to catch our attention, and refuse to consider it any further. Only after repeated, discouraging failures are some of us fortunate enough to pause, and give proper consideration to an important something that we had previously dismissed out of hand.

Often, this pause comes as a reaction to our having noticed on the horizon a signpost telling us that we've been working away at our worlds for a surprising length of time, and that the only certainty regarding the time remaining to us is that it is not unlimited. A serious illness can be such a signpost. So can a fortieth birthday receding into the distance, while a fiftieth comes increasingly into focus ahead. Our discomfort heightens. Our vague anxiety clarifies into a single thought, one which we can no longer tuck quietly away. *We're on the wrong track.*

But where *is* the right track? How do we get onto it? And — most disconcerting of all — how will we know when we're there?

Actually, this last question is the easiest one to answer. When we are on the right track, we know it at once. All the senses are suddenly heightened. Colors and sounds are more vivid. Concentration is intensified. There is a strong sense of being involved in an interesting and worthwhile activity, and a feeling of unity with understanding colleagues from the past and the future, no less than with those from the present. Each of our actions and each personal interaction resonates with significance.

But how do we find our way onto this right track? Probably by taking first things first. To ride a track, you need a vehicle, and you can't ride the right track in the wrong vehicle. So, keep alert for the right vehicle, then, and as soon as you recognize it, jump aboard. Because whatever it may be — the teaching of reading, the practice of medicine, or the restoration of antique music boxes — if that vehicle really is the right one for you, you'll suddenly find yourself, without any further thought or effort, zipping smoothly along, barreling your way straight down the right track. Just like that.

Just like magic, you might say.

And at that point, it may occur to you that there really is only one right track. It's just that the number of right vehicles is endless.

Mechanical music carries me through my life. The sound of a fine music box is, for me, a specific antidote to the poisonous discouragement of that persistent, malicious questioner who insists upon asking what anything I may do will matter in a hundred, a thousand, or a million years. As long as the music keeps playing, the question falls flat on its irrelevance, and I proceed cheerfully along my way.

Not that I could even begin to say why the voice of mechanical music happened to be the catalyst which dissolved my perceptual limitations –- but magic understood is something other than magic. One simply accepts, and is grateful for the gift.

Once upon a time, very casually, it seemed, I put a music box into my world. But then, I discovered that there was a world within that music box.

Listen . . .

Who's That Knocking at My Door?

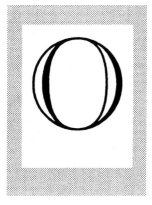

pportunity knocks only once, you say? Well, forget that; it's nonsense. The lady is forever banging away at our doors, driving us crazy with her interruptions — and that's the problem. She distracts us to fidgets: let her get just one foot in the door, and next thing she's trampling all over our carefully settled plans. Better to do without her encyclopedias or scrubbrushes, or whatever it is she's trying to peddle. So, we tell her to get lost, slam the door in her face, and then go on about whatever our dreary business of the moment may be.

But Opportunity is a saleslady through and through. She never gives up on a prospect. As long as you're there to answer, she'll be calling on you. She's got faith in her product; she knows you'll buy, if only she can get that foot in the door, and keep it there long enough to snatch your attention. She knows just what it is you can not live without, and her merchandise never changes — it's only the sales pitch that varies.

Not many of these pitches succeed, though. When things are going well for us, we're usually too impatient to grant her the time of day, and when things are going badly, we're so tired and discouraged that listening seems pointless. But every now and again, our luck comes through. Opportunity tosses out just the right line for the moment, and after an instant of stupefaction, we cry, "Huzzah!" and congratulate ourselves on our perspicuity. And Opportunity rolls her eyes, and wonders why in the name of anything holy she persists at this line of work. A thankless job!

When I was seven years old, my favorite toy was a little wind-up phonograph, a child's model, small enough for a munchkin to drag around by its leather handle. It was covered with white cloth on which had been printed scenes of nursery rhyme characters at play. Humpty Dumpty, that cheery-faced egghead, sat unsuspecting on his wall, while the king's horses and the king's men bided their time below, waiting for the command to resume their Sisyphean occupation. Anguished Jill clutched her temples over fallen Jack, wondering how she was ever going to make it all those years as a widow on Social Security. And Old King Cole lounged gracefully in his chair, puffing at his pipe with all the insouciance of a college sophomore, as he nodded with clear approval at the antics of the royal string trio. This one was my favorite. "Stay tuned!" I would say to my audience. "In a minute, we'll be hearing the latest hit from Old King Cole and His Fiddlers Three."

Of course, that hit was never heard by my vast horde of listeners: there was no such group and no such song. If I had been born a decade later, I probably would have worked Nat King Cole into the routine — but then again, if I'd been born ten years later, I probably would not have had the wind-up phonograph in the first place.

Still, I couldn't complain. At a mere seven years of age, I was at the top of my profession. My audience was the biggest in the New York-New Jersey-Connecticut listening area; every morning and every afternoon, millions of people tuned their radios to WPAT (There really *was* such a station, the voice of Paterson, New Jersey) for the "Listen to Laurence" Show. And what they heard was not nursery rhymes, either. If I ever actually owned any children's records, I don't recall them, nor do I recall ever playing them. What I do remember was Duke Ellington Taking the A Train. And Sammy Kaye (with his happy-go-lucky Kaydets) Taking a Chance on Love. Bing telling the Andrews Sisters not to Fence him In. Russ Morgan Dancing With A Dolly With a Hole in Her Stocking. Bea Wain and her gorgeous Deep Purple voice, Double-Daring us to fall in love with her. And of course, Spike Jones, even a year after V-E Day, now, still and forever firing! firing! Right in Der Fuehrer's Face.

My listeners got the biggest hits of the year, you'd better believe it. I'd drive my mother crazy until finally, she'd give up and take me downtown to Landay's Music Shop, where I'd pick out two or three records. I knew which ones to buy because I'd heard them on the radio. When I wasn't on the air myself, I was listening to the competition.

How does it happen that a seven-year-old kid comes to spend all these hours on end playing disk jockey? Maybe it's just that people really do show their track early, and there are some of us who'll grab every available moment to blather away to anybody who'll lend even half an ear. Maybe so. Maybe also, in this case, it had to do with the fact that I stuttered so badly I literally could not speak a coherent sentence, even in the most casual conversation –- and, to make matters worse, my would-be listeners sometimes pointed fingers at me and laughed. Damn it to hell, there had to be *some* audience I could talk to.

From the word go, the "Listen to Laurence Show" was pure let-me-entertain-you. I had nothing in particular to sell. There were no words from any sponsors, no commentary on the news. Neither was I a fledgling show-biz groupie. I couldn't have told you the first thing about which singer was married to which bandleader, or which number husband that was for her. It never occurred to me that these performers might actually have had lives off the record.

What mattered to me was the music. I was crazy for music. Without music, life plodded along in sad, dull shades of black and white, but just let there be music, and the technicolor projectors started to roll. My favorite singer was Bing Crosby, because his voice was such a wonderful shade of rich, dark brown, swirling in delightfully smooth, ever-changing patterns on a white background. Sort of like hot fudge melting into vanilla ice cream. Harriet Hilliard was cool peppermint-green columns, waxing and waning, flowing and dripping, the most marvelous sort of refreshment for a hot, summer mood. And Bea Wain! Bea Wain was an endless curtain of lush purple velvet, rippling and fluttering as if in a breeze, as the pitch of her voice rose and fell. The first time I ever heard Bea Wain sing, "When the deep purple falls, over sleepy garden walls," every square millimeter of my skin popped out in goose pimples. If I had been older, I'd have made some sort of observation about life imitating art, but being seven years old, I was content to simply luxuriate in the vision.

Best of all, though, were the instrumental pieces: all rich, gorgeous brocades springing up full-stitched, and then evolving before my eyes. Subtle musical transitions produced minor pattern changes, while the sudden entry of a new section of the orchestra would shift the entire weave, color, and texture of the work. Violins set up patterns in tiny threads; woodwinds produced thicker ribbons. Most wonderful were the brasses. The more trumpets, the more intense the golden glow that illuminated the fabric. This kid would have walked all day and night to listen to a Louis Armstrong riff. And trombones were super –- when Kid Ory let go, it was as if he were beaming a giant stage lamp onto the production, causing all the colors to shine forth with an almost-unnatural power, while the entire warp and weft pulsated gently back and forth in front of my staring eyes.

So, it was the music — but it was also the crank. Remember the crank? Mine was an old, *wind-up* phonograph, and part of the DJ's responsibility was to provide the energy that would keep his show on the air. Of course, as he listened to his favorite performers, the visions would distract him so that all of a sudden, the record would be turning at perhaps 60, or even 50, rpm. You know what this does to the sound. The effect on the colored visions was to create a very similar distortion; overall, the effect was like that of a funhouse mirror. This was pleasant, and made the young DJ giggle. But duty invariably called, so that after a moment or two of stolen pleasure, he'd quickly wind the crank, and offer a brief apology to the undoubtedly-distracted audience. Wind and listen; wind, announce the title, and listen.

Then, one afternoon, right in the middle of a wind, the phonograph suffered a sudden, fatal heart attack. The loud snap as the spring broke threw my life utterly out of kilter. When my father suggested getting rid of the machine and buying a new one, I threw the tantrum of my short life. So, Pop quickly promised to get the damn thing fixed. He took it down to Ben Merker's radio repair shop.

The week that passed until the machine was ready may have been the longest seven days that either of my poor parents ever knew. When Pop finally came through the door with the phonograph tucked under his arm, I leaped from his chair with a howl.

But then, I stopped cold. The phonograph was altered. There was an electric cord hanging from it.

"Ben put a motor in it," Pop said. He was all smiles. "Look." He set the phonograph down on the floor, and plugged it in. Then, he pushed a button on the line cord, and the turntable started to spin. "See," he said. "Now, you don't have to keep winding it up. And it'll always play at the right speed."

I stared at the empty crank hole. "What did Mr. Merker do with the crank?" I asked.

"I don't know," Pop said. "Threw it away, I guess. Why?"

"Nothing," I said, but I was lying. I knew right then, even before I tried it, that it was no good. The crank hole had the appearance of a gaping wound, and the missing speed-control lever gave the impression of a grotesque deformity. It had been fun to fiddle with that thing while a record was playing, so as to give my listeners the pleasure of hearing a serial duet by, say, Vaughn Monroe and Donald Duck. But now, all I could do was push the button on the line cord, let the record play, and then push the button the other way to turn it off. Which I did, once or twice. But that was all the time it took me to realize that I had lost my audience. They'd deserted me for Martin Block and Ted Husing and Jack Lacy. Not that I could really blame them. My show had lost its life; the musical colors had faded and gone dull. I hid the phonograph at the back of my closet, under a pile of books and records. Though Pop's obvious confusion and annoyance made me feel bad — I understood that he had, after all, been trying to do a nice thing for me — it made me feel even worse to play, or play with, my mutilated machine. "Listen to Laurence" never again graced the airwaves.

As I look back from my present vantage point, I can clearly see Opportunity pounding away at my door. "Hey, kid," she's shouting. "Have I got a deal for you!" But not many seven year olds could have had the savvy to realize that this was not just another one of those commonplace sweet-talkers of everyone's childhood — just one more con artist trying to peddle brummagem and bogus goods to little kids. I can't really fault myself for turning my back, and going on about my business.

My next knock, a harder one, came some eight, largely black-

and-white years later. My family always spent the last two weeks in August at the seashore; this year, it was Asbury Park. Days, we spent on the beach and in the water; then, in the evenings, after dinner, my parents would rock in the wicker chairs on the hotel porch, and I would strike out on my own to walk along the board-walk.

The sun was setting earlier now, and the air was noticeably cooler than at this time of night in July. In just a few days, Asbury would be a ghost town until the next spring — all the amusement casinos boarded up, the salt water taffy machines immobile. Out on the darkening water, I could make out large boats, probably steamers. On their way to Hong Kong, maybe, or Calcutta. It would be neat, I'd sometimes think, to take a ride on one of them before winter came and socked everything in.

I'd walk down to the casino, and play a few games of skee-roll; then, I'd go back out on the boards and stare at the pretty girls, blonde and suntanned, in their short, white dresses. But the skee-ball was no more than a light pastime, and as for the pretty girls — - well, where the blue of the night was meeting the gold of the day on the Asbury Park boardwalk, it was definitely not me that these chicks were waiting for. No way. By fifteen, I'd already had enough anxiety-laced giggles and pointed fingers to last me a lifetime. When your vocal carburetor floods at less than the least provoca-tion, you might as well just admit you're dead at the side of the road, and start hiking.

Usually, I'd hike up to the auction.

There was a little auction gallery, right on the Asbury Park boardwalk. Its name was Richard Kadrey's, and their stuff, as I recall it, ran heavily to nineteenth-century furniture and Persian rugs. It was fun to stand among the crowd in the doorway and watch the bidding, and although I often thought about trying to get a better look, I was reluctant to go inside and sit down. For one thing, they might have asked me whether I wanted a bidding paddle, and then I'd have had to say, "N-n-n-n-no, th-th-thanks." Also, the people in the place had a decidedly dangerous appear-ance — which was probably because the massed body heat brought out the grease on their faces, and the cigarette smoke, thick enough to induce immediate pulmonary neoplasia at the first innocent inhalation, was making them squint. But these fine points didn't occur to me. All I could think was, what if I should sit down next to the wrong man, feel a sharp jab in my thigh, and then wake up at sea, aboard one of those tramp steamers that looked like they'd be so much fun to hitch a ride on? No thanks. The doorway was close enough.

Except for one time. It was the Labor Day Weekend, Saturday night, I think. The last auction of the season. It was a real New Jersey summer night, the air classifiable as a potable beverage. Inside the gallery, women were everywhere working their fans, and even in the doorway, the heat and humidity were stifling. Perspiration poured down my face; my light shirt stuck to my chest and back. Still, I had no thoughts of leaving. What would I do –- sit with my parents and the other older people on the hotel porch? You'd have to be kidding! And it was no less hot in the arcades and casinos. Besides, how many skee-balls can you roll in an evening? How long can you stand watching a human mural of adenoidally expectant faces at a wheel of fortune, hoping at 35 to 1 that a little white ball will just happen to drop into a slot marked by a particular number?

No, the auction was the best show in town, the weather notwithstanding. The bidding was lively that night, even frenzied in spots. Maybe this had to do with its being the last sale of the season — one of those Last Chance Phenomena. People were paying unthinkable sums of money — hundreds, even thousands of dollars — for oil paintings, and rugs, and bedroom sets. Who *had* this kind of money to spend? Not anyone I knew.

Then, it happened. The auctioneer pointed to a wooden box up on a table. I'd looked at it from time to time during the evening, wondering what it might be. By shape, it suggested a coffin, but one for a decidedly small person, someone perhaps four or four and a half feet tall. But none of the few coffins I'd seen had been so nicely decorated as this one: lovely designs of brass and different colors of wood were inlaid over both lid and front. And the table appeared to match the box in every respect.

An assistant opened the lid, which didn't help me much. I could make out some sort of shiny metal plate inside the lid, but from the doorway, I could not see down into the box. The auctioneer began to speak. "Number 245," he intoned. "Genuine Swiss music box, and oh yes, it's a bee-*yoo*-tiful one, let me tell you. Almost one hundred years old now, it is, and in perfect working condition. Brought over from Europe by the grandfather of the present owner, as a wedding gift for his new bride."

The assistant pulled open the drawer at the front of the table. Something inside gleamed bright yellow.

"Comes with six — that's right, six — brass music drums, each one with absolutely the finest kind of music," the auctioneer cried. He looked down at the machine. "Benny, let's show the people what this little beauty sounds like."

Benny was grinning. He pulled at a lever to the right, inside the box.

There was no way I could have prepared myself for what happened then. Into the low buzz of the gallery conversation burst an explosion of color, dense enough to filter the auctioneer, the crowd, the artifacts — *everything* — down to the merest shadows. This was music the likes of which I'd never seen before, nor could I have imagined. The tune was *Carnival of Venice*, which I'd heard many times, but never in a manner remotely resembling this. I'd once read a story in which one of the characters made reference to the tinkly sound of an old music box, but the sounds I was hearing resembled that description about as well as the discharge of a cannon ball resembles the firing of a popgun. There was blue; there was red; and yellow. Colors blended and multiplied; primaries, secondaries, tertiaries all flowed together and then worked their way back apart. A trill of high-pitched notes shot a punctate orange ribbon through the middle of the vision. It was a rainbow poured into a giant Waring blender, then sent flowing generously down before me. The vivid panorama swirled in the dense air; it rose and it fell. A louder passage of music intensified the colors, and they moved forward to wrap themselves around me. I was Joseph, in his multicolored coat, wearing that dangerous gift from a loving father. My face radiated heat, and, it seemed, light, back into the night.

Then, the music stopped. My colored coat was suddenly gone, and I found myself leaning against the man to my right, laboring to draw breath. The man said something I couldn't hear, made a disgusted face, and shoved me away, not gently. Without any thought,

I moved in the direction of his push, so that I was standing in the entry aisle to the gallery, still at the rear, but at this moment, definitely inside.

"Now, ladies and gentlemen," the auctioneer said. "What else can I say, after you've heard that. Who'll start the bidding at one hundred dollars? One hundred! . . . No? Well, who'll bid fifty then; fifty dollars for this magnificent Swiss music box, with six cylinders of music? Fifty, fifty, fifty . . . All right, then. Twenty-five! Twenty-five dollars. Come on, ladies and gentlemen."

I saw two paddles go up, one in front of me to the left, one to the right. The auctioneer's voice was a pale, crumbly dirty yellow, so revolting by contrast to the glorious sound of the music box that I became nauseated.

I wiped my hands on my shirt front; they came away dripping. Slowly, I worked my way forward, up the aisle, until at last I was standing before the music box. Now, I could see inside. I stared at the bright, steel teeth of the comb, and the gleaming brass of the cylinder and the spring barrel. Benny was still at the controls, and I looked at him as I thought, Play it! Start it up again!

He grinned at me through a set of very bad teeth. "Go ahead, kid," he whispered hoarsely. "Bid on it. You kin buy it. Just raise up your hand."

A couple of drops of perspiration wrung themselves from the pores of my forehead, and splatted onto the teeth of the comb. I WANTED that music box! I ached for it. I would wind it up, turn it on, and never let it run down. I'd fill the air with its music. I'd broadcast it around the world.

But the bidding was now up to one hundred dollars. What was I, crazy? A hundred dollars: a week's pay for my father. Two months' rent. A month of food. What was I going to do — pledge a hundred dollars, and then try to explain to my father why he should lend me that money till I could get to my bank account?

But how could I just up and walk away from this incredible music machine?

At that point, somebody bid $125, and this gave the decisive tip to my little scale of ambivalence. Plainly put, I turned and ran. On all sides I saw little white bubbles of laughter, growing, popping, and then springing back into existence. I brushed them away from my face as I charged out onto the boardwalk. By some very fancy footwork, I managed to avoid crashing into a wicker sightseeing carriage; the lap-robed old couple clucked and shook their heads as I barreled past them, up the boards, to finally collapse on an unoccupied bench facing out to sea.

As soon as I sat down, I wanted to run right back, but I knew my decision was already irrevocable. By now, the music box would be sold, and even if it were not, I was hardly about to raise my hand to offer two hundred dollars, or even more. I didn't want to think about what my parents would say –- and really, who could blame them? They worked hard and long for that kind of money. We were not poverty cases, but we certainly weren't wealthy people, either. We did not have money to squander on expensive luxuries –- and in our home, an old music box was far from a necessity!

By the time I started walking back to the hotel, I was convinced I'd done the right thing. Sure, I had a bank account with several hundred dollars of summertime earnings in it, and yes, that money was mine to do with as I pleased. But I had determined to go to medical school, and that was not going to be an inexpensive proposition.

It might have occurred to me then to notice that I was making quite a point of going back along the city streets, rather than the boardwalk, so as to avoid having to walk past the auction gallery, where I might possibly see someone carrying my music box out. How certain *was* I that I'd made the proper decision?

But these thoughts never entered my head. Earlier that spring, when my high school advisor had asked me about my career plans, and I'd said that, well, I thought maybe I might become a doctor, she had raised her eyebrows and shaken her head vigorously. No, she told me with all the certainty that a twenty-five year old girls' gym teacher can put forth; no, that was *not* a good idea. Not with *my* stutter. Why, I shouldn't even *think* of doing that. What if, say, I were in an operating room, and needed to ask for a particular instrument, and I couldn't, and the patient died?

It was at that moment that my tentative idea became cast in concrete. What did she *mean*, I couldn't? Or shouldn't? By God, I just jolly well *would*, if I wanted! I began my journey into the healing arts by stomping out of the counseling room, and refusing ever to go back.

So it just plain didn't matter that I liked that music box. I couldn't buy it; that was all. I couldn't *afford* to buy it. I was very pleased with myself for being such a thoroughly sensible fellow.

Opportunity, on the other hand, must have put me down as one of history's great fools, suffering from a deafness far more damaging than Beethoven's. Her knuckles must have given her pain for weeks.

Fortunately, though, the lady didn't give up on me. All through college, there she was, tapping away with both patience and persistence. Look how much you enjoy your music courses, she kept saying. And how you really get turned on in the English classes. But biology is so tedious, and chemistry is to be barely endured. And physics at best is agony. Hey! Wake up, would you? Stop and think for a minute.

But I just kept telling her to go away and leave me alone. Premed students have no time for sirens. I don't *want* to stop and think, I insisted. I'm going to be a doctor.

By the time I got to medical school, the knocks had become fainter, and far fewer in number. I thought maybe I'd worn my intruder down, but of course it was no such thing. Wiser than I all along, she simply knew when to bide her time. She let me go on, pretty much undisturbed, through med school, internship, residency, and some thirteen painfully black and white years of work as an obstetrician.

And at that point, she must have decided it was time to make another call on the hardhead. Maybe by now, he'd be ready to listen.

Was he ever.

The knock came on a Sunday afternoon in June, 1983. My wife, our two kids, and I had gone up to Vancouver, British Columbia, for a long weekend of museums, window-shopping, and food. On Sunday, shortly before it was time to start back, we were strolling through Gastown, Vancouver's former skid-row region, now reclaimed for the tourist crowd. Filthy dives had been upgraded to high-toned French restaurants; cheap hotels to antiques shops. My interest in antiques, I would have told you then, was nonexistent, but that was all right. For a couple of hours' diversion, this would be okay.

On the way back to the car, we cut through a corner building, a huge, barn-like place all full of pieces of furniture with numbered tags on them. If I was thinking about anything in particular, I don't recall it, but suddenly I realized that I was standing still, fixed and fixated on a crank. This winding handle was protruding from the side of a rather plain, mahogany-stained upright phonograph.

"Hey, look," I finally said. But my family had already gone on ahead.

I gave the crank a wind, placed the needle onto the record that was sitting on the turntable, and released the brake. Immediately, the room was filled with the boopy-doopy-doopy sound of a British dance orchestra of the 1930s.

It's a great temptation to put down here that instantly, I was overpowered by a marvelous vision of the past, that a giant flying carpet of gorgeous colors returned me to the Listen to Laurence Show, and that in that perfect moment of revelation and understanding, I decided to return to Seattle, close my medical office first thing in the morning, and sign on as a deejay for one of the local radio stations. I won't say that, though, because there wouldn't be a particle of truth in it, and so, it would also be lousy fiction. In point of fact, the colors, though a pleasant tandem of green and gold sine waves, were quite faint, owing both to the scratchiness of the record and to my own longstanding disuse atrophy. In addition, I had no thoughts whatever about being a real disk jockey; in that regard, my former high school advisor would have been justified in questioning my judgement. My stutter would have made such a pursuit about as reasonable for me as a four-minute mile run for a one-legged man. And in any event, Listen to Laurence was just about the farthest thing right then from my conscious mind; that particular association didn't occur to me until years later.

All I knew was that I wanted to take that phonograph home.

Which, at that moment, was all Opportunity was asking of me. "You want to take *this* home?" said my wife.

Hearing the music, my family had come back to see what in hell Dad had gotten into now. The expression on my wife's face suggested that she certainly hoped I was kidding, but really, what sort of joke was this?

"Well, yes," I said. "*Listen* to it. Isn't it neat?"

"If you say so," said Myra. Her expression made it clear that *she* didn't.

I lifted the needle from the record, and turned off the machine. "I don't see a price tag," I said. I'm going to go find out what it'd cost."

I started walking toward the little, glassed-in office at the far end of the huge room.

"Where are you going to get records to play on it?" Myra called after me. "They don't make 78s any more."

I shrugged and kept walking. How did I know where I was going to get records? One thing at a time.

The little fellow in the office scratched at his cap and gave me an odd look when I inquired as to the price of the phonograph. "This's an auction house, Mate," he said. "Auction's tomorra night."

Here, I might invoke an image of a long-ago evening on the boardwalk at Asbury Park, the air heavy with moisture and portents — but once again, I'll restrain myself. The only thought I had right at that moment was that I lived and worked in Seattle, 150 miles away, and there was no way on earth I could get back for this auction. All I could say was, "You mean I can't just . . . buy it, then? I mean, buy it *now*?"

In retrospect, I have to say that the little man's patience was exemplary. "No, mate, y'can't," he said. "See, it's an auction. You know –- people come and they bid on these things. Person makes the highest bid, they're the one who takes it home. So, why don't you just come back tomorra, see? When the auctioneer puts up that grammyphone, why then, you just bid on it. And if y' want it more'n anyone else here, why, it'll be yours. See?"

I thanked him, and we left. Myra, I will say, was properly sympathetic. "I'm sorry you couldn't buy that machine, if you really did like it so much," she said.

"I'll get another one," I told her. "If there's one around, there's really got to be another."

I suspect my wife thought that by the next morning, I'd be back into the routine, and the phonograph would be forgotten. She was only half-right, though –- the first half. As I went about my business, I found I could think of nothing beyond that silly phonograph. It struck me as odd behavior, to say the least, but I had not the slightest inclination to resist it.

Which must have pleased poor, persistent, sore-knuckled Opportunity no end.

For three weeks, I thought about the phonograph, and then, as I was driving with Myra along 45th Street in Seattle, I caught a glimpse of another phonograph, standing in a shop window. By reflex, I zipped the VW across the path of a giant Pepsi truck, and into the parking space that had obviously been reserved for me in front of the store.

My wife's opinion of my driving skills is about on a level with a snake's gizzard, and she is not bashful about making me aware of this. Usually, I can offer something in the way of a reasoned response, but this time, all I could do by way of attempted exculpation, was to point at the extenuating circumstances in the window.

When people manage to stay married for twenty-one years, it's usually at least partly because they've got some idea of when to keep their mouths shut. Myra interrupted her lecture, and followed me quietly into the store, where, for $125, I ransomed my treasure. She was a staid, upright, mahogany Columbia Grafonola — quite similar in appearance, actually, to the Vancouver machine, and not exactly the sort of phonograph to set the heart of a seasoned collector aquiver. But this I didn't know. Like Frederic in *The Pirates of Penzance*, I had precious little basis for comparative evaluation, and so, my own cardiac rhythm was severely disrupted. And unlike Frederic, I was not distracted by the timely arrival of the fair daughters of a Modern Major General; thus, my phonographic Ruth came home with me, along with half a hundred of those scratchy but highly nostalgiagenic 78 rpm records, courtesy of the generous antiques dealer.

All the time this business was taking place, I was operating under the assumption that my phonograph was no more than an impulse purchase –- one of those infrequent deviations from my customary sober and responsible attitude toward money. Just one of those bells that now and then rings . . . But it didn't quite work out that way. I listened to my records, and then went out and bought some more. I found out that there were books about old phonographs, so I bought and read them. And then I discovered that there were some people around who actually collected (Can you *believe* such a thing?) these machines — so I went to visit them and see their stuff. It was incredible! These guys had rooms lined with phonographs. They had closets bursting with them. Their garages were impassable; their basements and attics were solid. You couldn't claw your way through. And of course, they all had one or two machines they'd be willing to sell . . .

So, in my case, the fair maidens had only been delayed. Once they arrived, though, I realized that I was a collector, and a serious one at that. Certainly not a sober one, though. And definitely not responsible. Within a surprisingly short time, a goodly number of the maidens managed to take up residence in my house, where their lovely oak or mahogany cases and their graceful horns made it painfully evident just *how* plain and ordinary Ruth was. Before long, my first love was singing her songs for someone else.

The paths traveled by collectors are numerous and full of inter-sections; consequently, I became increasingly aware that such things as music boxes existed. In fact, I even bought one — a little hand-cranked Regina that played sprightly, bell-like music from eight-inch discs of zinc or steel. But I was not going to collect them: so I told Myra. Too expensive; just too much money. Why, for the price of just one music box, a person could buy ten phonographs. Which remark, I immediately realized, was a major tactical error. Myra glanced as though by reflex at her poor, cramped Wedgwood collection, squeezed and rammed into every possible cranny in the dining room, and then she started to count the phonographs in the living room.

"Oh, I don't know," she said. "I think I just might like music boxes."

After twenty-odd (take that as you will) years of marriage, one learns to both recognize spousespeak, and regard it with proper seriousness. I quietly, but very firmly, determined that my token music box would remain exactly that.

So, there I went again — lowering my shoulder and putting it to the door. Better to shut off that pest of an itinerant saleslady before she can even open her mouth. After thirty years of practice, I'd gotten pretty good at it, but this time, the advantage was definitely with Opportunity. All the time she'd been going on about phonographs, I had never even stopped to consider that this might be only the loss leader, just a setup to allow her to slip in the real sales pitch from the blind side. And now, her foot was through the door; she was not about to pull it back. Not with a sure sale one more knock away. She clenched her fingers and cocked her fist. She was ready, at last, for the knockout knock.

A couple of weekends later, she delivered it. As Myra and I walked into a local antiques show, I heard a music box playing somewhere across the room. What a wonderful sound! I nudged my wife. "Think I'll go see what that *is*," I said, trying to sound tentative.

A scheming spouse, however, is not the best person to apply to for aid; she had not the slightest intention of lashing me to the mast. "Fine," she said cheerfully. "I'll catch up with you."

Thus abandoned by my crew, I set off in the direction of the siren. She was perched on a glass showcase at the front of a booth, and was as lovely to the eye as she'd been to the ear. She was cloaked in a lustrous garment of rosewood, with eye-grabbing wooden inlays and banding. Inside, she was all shiny nickeled metal. Within the lid was a colorful tune card, labelled SUBLIME HARMONIE, and listing the six airs that comprised her repertoire. As I approached, she was singing Mendelssohn's *Spring Song*.

The music was unlike any I'd ever heard from any source, save one — a certain machine in an auction gallery in Asbury Park, one hot and humid evening, three decades before. Even in that huge gymnasium where the antiques show was being held, the sound was bright, clear, and rich. The arrangements were full of the most marvelous, intricate embellishments: arpeggios and appogiaturas; trills and short mandolin-like passages; crescendoes and runs sweeping along the entire length of the comb.

Although the room was not particularly warm, I was suddenly soaked with sweat. That gorgeous voice had taken silk as blue as the night and as gold as the day, and spun it out in a web around me. The fabric was as strong as it was delicate, each note seeming to draw me closer and closer to the spinner. With some difficulty, I looked past the singer to the elderly couple behind the counter. "Where did you *get* this?" I asked.

"It *is* a beautiful one, isn't it?" the woman said. She was smiling, that antique-dealer look that says, *You* know you're hooked, and *I* know you're hooked. And *you* know that *I* know, but so what?

"We got it last month at an auction in Philadelphia," said her husband. "We thought we just *had* to buy it. It's the nicest music box we've ever seen."

"Would you mind . . . playing it again for me?" I asked.

"Not at all." The woman gave the winding lever a few pulls, and pushed the start lever.

I held my breath. It won't sound as good the second time through, I thought, and in a sense I was right. It sounded even better.

As the machine was winding down, Myra came up. "Oh, isn't that a pretty one," she said.

"Could you play it again?" I asked, and then added, quickly, "So my wife can hear it."

The woman smiled again — grinned, actually — and once again set the box into motion. Streams of perspiration were carving paths down my forehead. I'd never seen a price tag on a phonograph to match the one on the lid of this music box. But I'd also never heard a phonograph that sounded even remotely like this music box. While it was playing, it would have been impossible for me to move, but when the woman shut it off, and the web of blue and gold faded away, I thanked her and began to walk away with Myra.

"Don't you want to buy it?" Myra said.

I muttered something about having to think it over.

"If somebody comes up and buys it while you're thinking," said my wife, "I expect I'm going to have to stand around and watch you, down on the floor, chewing the legs off their display cabinet."

Ambrose Bierce is said to have remarked that when the devil needed some help getting a job done, he called in a woman. Perhaps he and Opportunity went to the same school. I turned around, and as if shot from a cannon, was back at the music box. The dealer laughed. "Turn it on yourself," she said. "You know how, don't you?"

That did it. The instant the music stopped, I pulled out my checkbook, and began to scribble. This sale had to be consummated, and quickly.

The old man reached over the counter to pat me on the shoulder. "I'm glad it's gonna go where somebody's gonna appreciate it," he said.

Which it certainly did. The music box sat in our musical place of honor, on the living-room coffee table. For some thousand and one nights she sang to us, while hordes of her sisters assembled around her, displacing the phonographs to other rooms and other homes. Though some of these new arrivals were of the type that played music from metal discs, most were cylinder music boxes, and most of these were early ones, made not later than the middle of the nineteenth century. Disc box music is pleasant enough, but I very shortly discovered that in the voice of a fine cylinder, one hears another entire dimension. The advantage of the disc box is that a greater number of tunes may be played; however, any one disc has much the same effect upon my ear as any other. These discs were machine-punched by the thousands, and to me, that's the way they sound. But no two cylinders have ever sounded the same to me, nor have any two airs on a particular cylinder. In the musical tone and in the arrangements of any of these individually-crafted masterpieces, I realized that I was hearing the voice of the maker, clear and undisciplined by reason, giving flight to every passion in the rainbow of emotion as he broadcast his fears and his anxieties, his loves and his wild hopes, down the dark, narrow corridors of time.

But soon or late, there's always trouble in Paradise. A Nicole Frères fat-cylinder overture box swept into the house, and demanded that coffee-table seat. Nowhere else would do. This was a nonnegotiable demand.

Now, in music boxes as in opera, fat is not in any way to be deprecated. The greater the diameter of the cylinder, the greater the number of pins that can be set into its surface. And since each pin represents one note of music, all else being equal, the fatter the cylinder, the more intricate the musical arrangement. Thus, a cylinder box that plays six magnificent selections from operatic overtures is in every regard a *prima donna*, and needs to be treated as such. So, for three days, I *schlepped* Nicole through the three floors of rooms in the house: perhaps I could interest her in another location. But she only sulked. Here, she wouldn't fit; there, she couldn't be reached for winding or playing. And everywhere, she was being placed beneath her proper station.

At last, I gave up, and took my First Box off the coffee table. I told myself that her new location in the Upstairs Music-Machine Room was perfectly fine, but as time passed, I felt increasingly uneasy. Why did I always have to play her *before* the Malignon box, with its elegant forte-piano combs and tuned, hidden bells — never after? Why did she look and sound so small opposite the big Bremond interchangeable-cylinder mandoline box? And why was I dusting her lid so much more frequently than I was opening it?

Finally, one day I admitted to myself that my poor First Box just didn't sound so good any more. What I was hearing when I pushed the start lever was falling progressively shorter of expectations. The thought that I might already be jaded was disconcerting, but I dismissed that idea: the First Box was an awfully good one, but she just was not in the class of the later arrivals. Which, I realized, really was to take nothing away from her. When I let my First Box play in the sound chamber of my imagination, I heard her just the way she'd sounded to me the day I bought her. Her voice had become the standard by which I judged all other music boxes *on first performance*. I looked around my music room. Not many machines had even come close, let alone actually met the test. But when one did, then I knew I had a real treasure.

Now, I understood the situation better still. Opportunity is always selling, but she's also forever buying. That's part of the act: after all, who can do business with an empty shop? So, if I were smart, I'd be listening with the proper degree of attention to every knock.

Thus, it happened that a couple of months later, when Myra and I left for the big annual mechanical music show and sale in Union, Illinois, the First Box was in the van, her case carefully wrapped. At the show, a stocky young man came up as she was playing; he listened through the entire program. I recognized the expression on his face, not because I'd seen it before, but because I'd felt it. As the box wound down, the man continued to stare. I wound it again; he thanked me. When the box stopped playing again, the man walked slowly away.

A short while later, he was back; he asked whether he might hear the music box again. "You can turn it on yourself," I said. "It's wound."

Again, the young man listened through the program, all the while staring with that same expression, but not saying a word. As I reached over to give the box another wind, I said to him, "I think you may have to take that music box home with you."

"I think you're right," he said, and laughed. He reached into his pocket.

I asked him what other music boxes he had.

He shook his head. "This's going to be my first," he said. "Oh, I've got some phonographs . . . but this one's my first music box."

"Is that so?" I said. "Well, I do hope you'll enjoy it every bit as much as I have."

"I'm sure I will," he said. "I really like it — I've never heard anything that sounds like it does . . . do you know what I mean?"

I knew very well indeed, but I just said yes. It would not have been fair to tell him that I hoped he wasn't overly attached to his phonographs.

As we were driving away from Union Sunday evening, Myra said, "You're not really happy about selling that box, are you?"

I shook my head.

"You shouldn't have done it, then," she said. "You didn't *have* to sell it."

I just grunted. No, I didn't *have* to, but yes, I *did* have to — but just how do you go about explaining to your wife that Opportunity buys *and* sells? That she's *always* buying and selling? Always buying and selling . . .

A few lines of poetry by William Carlos Williams popped into my head. Williams was a doctor-poet from New Jersey, and his major work bore as its title the name of my home town, Paterson. In Book II of this very long poem, Williams stated:

No defeat is made up entirely of defeat –- since
the world it opens is always a place
    formerly
        unsuspected. A
  world lost,
    a world unsuspected
      beckons to new places

Doc Williams was a keen observer. I wondered how long it had taken him to understand the *modus operandi* of Miss Opportunity.

I glanced across the front seat at Myra. "You know what?" I said.

She replied with that wifely "Ye-e-e-s?", that pathologically stretched monosyllable that means, No, I *don't* know what, and if you really want to know the truth, I'm not sure I *want* to know what.

"Remember that incredible grande format music box we saw for sale a few months ago? The one that plays four overtures on a cylinder more than five inches thick?"

She nodded her head. All of a sudden she knew. "You can buy it, now, can't you?" she said. "Now, you've got the money."

"Yep," I said. "I think I'll call and do it first thing in the morning."

Knock, knock.

Nice Jewish Boys Can *So* Fix Music Boxes

or

Gloria in Extremis

robably the most fundamental work ethic of the North-Jersey Jewish society of my formative years was founded upon the conviction that work done with the mind was praiseworthy. Work done by hand, however, was worthy only of disdain. Why, anyone could do *manual labor* if they wanted to — but why would any person with a working brain ever want to? Like hiking into a swamp with a gun to blast ducks out of the sky, drinking beer in a crowded tavern on Saturday night, or going to the boxing matches, manual labor was looked upon as an activity with pleasures and rewards fixed squarely at Neanderthal level. At best, as a hobby, it was a waste of time. At worst, as a person's life's-work, it was no less than the waste of that life. This attitude ran deep. My friend Douggy came back from religious school one day and told me all about the way God had taken a lump of clay, worked it and shaped it with his hands, breathed life into it, and poof! *Ecce* Adam! Nonsense, I replied; it didn't happen that way. Not at all. God just said Let There Be, and there was. The same way He'd created the whole rest of the world. An act of pure Imagination become Reality by the direct mediation of Will.

Douggy, however, was not at all convinced. "That's the dumbest thing I ever heard," he shouted.

"Go look in the Bible," I told him. "You'll see. It doesn't say anything about shaping clay."

Douggy's response was to scream that I couldn't call *his* priest a liar; then, he punched me in the nose, which effectively ended the discussion but left the situation unaltered. On the Sabbath, the God of the Jews took a couple of aspirins and rested His aching head, while the Christian God plugged in the heating pad and rubbed Ben-Gay into His sore back.

My father set me a clear example. Pop was a college professor; he earned his living teaching young men and women to read effectively, and to understand and enjoy literature. He kept a small box of tools — a hammer, a couple of screwdrivers, a drill — sequestered in the farthest basement room, and he used them as infrequently as possible. And when he did, it was with the loudest possible protest, making it clear to all observers that he was acting under duress. The semiannual exchange of storm windows for screens was the nightmare of my teenage years: a full day of screaming, yelling, muttering, and cursing, culminating at dinnertime in the Father-and-Son Cut, Bruise, and Scrape Competition. And as for fixing something — well, the only such occurrence I can recall was the day the kitchen sink stopped up. As Pop returned from our next-door neighbor's, a pipe wrench in his hand, and his face like a Kansas sky a moment before a tornado, my Aunt Miriam clutched at her temples in mock dismay, and shouted "*Vay iz mir!*" My mother, in distress far more genuine, cried out, "Mark, for God's sake! Call the plumber!" Which, eventually, he had to do, and did.

So, I never learned how to unstop a clogged drainpipe. Or, for that matter, to stop a roof from leaking, build a fence or a stone wall in a garden, or bring the voice back to a silent radio. I never learned how to drive a screw cleanly, so as to leave its slot undamaged and pleasing to the eye. I never learned to drive a nail without leaving those depressed and depressing circular souvenirs of the hammerhead on the surrounding wood. With regard to this sort of work, my childhood lessons were more in the way of a single maxim. Which was: the more incompetent you are (or at least can appear to be) with your hands, the more brainy you must be (or at least will be considered to be).

I learned my lesson well. By my forty-fifth year, I had established the proud record of having not fixed or built a single thing in my life. In addition, I was pleasantly aware that my family and friends considered the placing of a hammer or a screwdriver into my hand to be an act of utter irresponsibility, something that only a dangerous lunatic might consider. By any imaginable criterion, I was a success.

But then came the music machines.

By the time I'd acquired my first few turn-of-the-century phonographs, I'd begun to realize that they didn't work nearly as well as they might. Forty years in a hot attic or a damp barn will do that. They needed work, but I couldn't exactly take them down to the TV and stereo repair shop, now, could I? So, I started to read about them –- not only their history, but also about how they were supposed to function. I found this to be not terribly painful; in fact (I had to admit, if very privately), it was even interesting. But when I'd sneak down to the cellar with a machine while my wife was away for a few hours, the situation immediately became hopeless. I had a vague idea that I really ought to have more tools than a hammer and a screwdriver and a drill, but that was not nearly my major problem. Literally, I did not know where to begin. These were simple machines, but not nearly as simple as I. Take out that screw, and loosen that nut? Me? Forget it. If I did, I'd be standing there with a handful of black, greasy chunks of metal, which would *never* go back together again. Not by anyone's efforts. The king's horses and men would consider Humpty-Dumpty a bargain by comparison. In a cold sweat, I'd quickly return to the living room, to go back to my book. What was I, crazy, to even think of doing such a thing? Better to just give the machines needing work to one of my new collector-friends, a nice fellow named Ed Curry, who had a fine workshop in his garage. For a very reasonable charge, Ed could make any phonograph play just fine.

So, I stuck to my last, reading and learning whatever I could keep in my head, and Ed made my phonographs functional for me. Every now and then, I'd clean and polish one, and the satisfaction I felt at the improvement in the appearance of the machine surprised me. Still, such a waste of time! I made certain to limit my silly puttering to, say, a couple of hours after I'd been at the hospital overnight, when I'd be too tired to accomplish anything worthwhile or productive, anyway. No point in just wasting that time altogether.

Then, I bought my first cylinder music box, a thing of beauty to eye and ear. But there was a problem. Even when I wound the spring fully, the machine ran for only a short time. Well, hundred-year-old springs do get weak, don't they? Fearing the worst, I took the box to another new friend, Bill Ullstrom; Bill restores and repairs music machines as a full-time retirement occupation. He took a quick look at my treasure, and announced that the Geneva was set wrong. To me, this pronouncement implied that at any moment, a small bomb might go off somewhere deep inside the machine, and blow it into the next century. But Bill did not appear in any way intimidated. He loosened a screw on the side of the spring barrel, gave a couple of turns to a small, nickeled component in the shape of a Maltese cross, and then retightened the screw. Now, the music box played through its full repertoire twice before running down.

I thanked Bill, and took the box home. A week and a half later, it wouldn't run at all. Back we went, the two of us, to the Music Box Doctor. Bill frowned slightly, as he studied the components he referred to as the governor. Then, he touched the long, narrow spout of the tiniest oil can I'd ever seen to one of the gears under his scrutiny, and voila! Music, music, music. "That was all it needed?" I said. "Just a drop of oil?"

Bill nodded. "The governor can get dry," he said. "Then, the box won't run. But it's important to put on only a tiny drop, and you should use the lightest oil you can get –- a good-grade clock oil, say. Otherwise, it only gets gummy, and then you've got to take it all apart and give the governor a good cleaning. That's more of a job."

Enough of a job, I was certain, to be forever beyond my capabilities. But still, I couldn't help thinking. It seemed crazy to have had to make two trips across Puget Sound on a ferryboat, first to have a screw loosened and tightened, and then to have a drop of oil applied to a gear. By now, I'd bought a second music box, and what did I intend to do: organize weekly Idiot Excursions to Port Orchard? And even if I did, how long could I reasonably expect Bill to continue to be as gracious with the Idiot as he had so far been?

There were other considerations as well. As I read my books

and magazines, and looked at increasing numbers of music boxes for sale, the thought intruded on me with increasing persistence that it would be nice to know — *really* know, and at first hand — how these machines worked. For one thing, I'd be much better equipped to properly evaluate a potential purchase, if I could make an intelligent estimate of its repair needs. Even more important, though, was a consideration more difficult to put in a straightforward fashion. The more I learned about music boxes, and the more I listened to them, the more convinced I became that by keeping myself ignorant of the mechanical and technical considerations, I was placing a major handicap in the way of my ability to appreciate the skill and the art of the particular geniuses who had created these wonderful musical contraptions. Put it this way: I could not have explained the function of the carburetor in a motor car, nor could I have identified a carburetor as it sat in its proper place in the engine. But that was all right: my car had never been more to me than a mode of transportation, a way to get from here to there. I had no particular desire to converse with Henry Ford. But for some reason, my heart was set upon being able to hear everything that David Lecoultre might have to say to me. Or Francois Nicole. Or any of the other early-nineteenth-century music box makers. And, increasingly, I became aware of how indistinct these voices could sometimes sound, the beauty and elegance of their creations notwithstanding. The problem, I knew, was with me. I needed to become more fluent in their language.

I set out to read all the repair advice I could find in the books and the journals, and I talked with Bill Ullstrom. I went out and bought a small music box to work on. If it had been a horse, they'd have shot it; if a human, they'd have pulled its plug without a second thought. There was no reason for me to feel intimidated, but I did anyway. Sure, I could take the thing apart, but then what? The chunks of brass, iron and steel in front of me bore only the most general resemblance to the pictures in the books. And the text was, effectively, a foreign language. Where does one even begin to know where to get a needle file, a center-punch, and a flexible-shaft tool? How does one begin to learn how to use them? As I stared at the greasy mess in front of me, I felt both helpless and discouraged. I had to learn this stuff, and by God, somehow I would. But how?

Finally, one November evening, Opportunity decided to favor my prepared mind. As I was reading the current issue of the Musical Box Society's *News Bulletin*, I came across the kind of information I'd been waiting for. Nancy Fratti and Joe Roesch, experts in the repair and restoration of cylinder music boxes, were announcing the opening of a school for restorers, to be held the following summer. For a solid five days, they would guide their students through the complete restoration procedure. Every aspect would be covered. And necessary tools would be furnished! "A-ha!" I shouted.

Myra looked at me with curiosity, tempered by just the proper degree of apprehension. "What's so interesting?" she asked.

I held out the page for her to see. At first, she looked puzzled, but then, realization hit. "Oh, you've got to be kidding," she said.

"Kidding?" I echoed. "Why?"

"Well, why don't we start with the fact that you don't know anything at all about repairing music boxes," she said.

"Fine," I told her. "That's true. But here's where I can find out. This is a school, isn't it? And they say right here that no prior knowledge is necessary — see?"

"Yes, I see," said my wife. "But usually when you apply to college, they figure that you've at least gotten through kindergarten."

"Very funny," I muttered.

But in the end, I had to concede that my lack of general background might in fact be a problem, so I sent off a quick letter to Nancy Fratti. "I don't know a ball-peen hammer from a bastard file," I wrote. "And although I really would like to learn to restore music boxes, there wouldn't be much point in my coming if all I'm going to do is waste your time and mine."

Nancy's reply arrived within a week. She professed to be mightily amused by my concern, and hastened to assure me that ball-peen hammers and bastard files are not even standard equipment for the music-box restorer. "If you have patience, and if you don't mind paying very careful attention to detail," she wrote, "you absolutely can learn to do most of the work in music-box restoration, and do it very well." She said that she and Joe would look forward to having me in attendance.

One Sunday evening the following August, I arrived at White-hall, New York, full of both unbridled enthusiasm and barely-contained terror. The thought occurred to me that it was unreasonable to suffer such anxiety. After all, wasn't I taught as a child that this was pretty simple stuff, involving only the most basic sort of skills? Hardly worthy of mention — wasn't that right? Well, if so, what was there to be so scared of? But I suppose that if we really could be so nicely analytical with ourselves, an awful lot of psychiatrists would be on food stamps.

I was one of a class of six, and although my five colleagues were as amiable as they could be, our get-acquainted dinner conversation did little toward easing my mind. These people were, every one of them, professionals or accomplished amateurs at restoration work. Two were clock and watch restorers; two were machinists; one was an all-round handyman of some fifty years' standing. They smiled when I said I had no knowledge whatever of repair work. They thought I was pulling their legs.

The following morning, however, as class began, they found out in a hurry that I had not been kidding in the least. Joe Roesch began by taking us through the orderly dismantling of a musical mechanism, and as I did what he told me to do with my sad little derelict, I wrote frantically in my notebook, knowing that I would never otherwise remember anything of the procedure. Often, I had to interrupt Joe's instructions to ask for a definition of what I knew was a very basic term.

As the hours passed, I realized to my astonishment that I was enjoying myself. I could easily have felt embarrassed by my ignorance, but my classmates would not permit that to happen. They all went out of their way to point things out to me, both saving me mistakes, and helping me to recover from ones I'd already made. No one ever sighed, snickered, or rolled his eyes when I asked how to read a micrometer, or what tempering was. And Joe Roesch turned out to be a superb teacher. A man just my own age, he was in fact a college professor of English — an irony not lost for an instant on me. Joe's command of language was no less than his mastery of tools and machines, and both were outstanding. In addition (thank God), he was patient. At one point, I apologized for the manner in which I had been using much more than my fair share of class time.

"Not at all," Joe told me. "These other fellows, I can't teach them anything, not really. They just need a little direction here, a word of advice there. But you! Now, *you* are someone I can really *teach*." It did not feel like a put-down, but even if it was, it was a mighty classy one, and I appreciated it.

School was scheduled from nine to five daily, but I usually worked till seven or eight in the evening. My notes grew, and so did my confidence. I learned the secrets of the balky governor, and familiarized myself with the erratic behavior of the superannuated coiled spring. I found out just what the Geneva stop mechanism was, and how to set it so that it would protect the spring from the hazards of either over- or underwinding. I learned how to properly polish brass and how to apply a protective lacquer coat. I straightened bent pins on the cylinder, so that they would strike the teeth cleanly, producing a sharp, clear note. I learned how to adjust and replace the tiny steel damper wires under the comb teeth, so the music would not be spoiled by squeaks, groans, and chirps. I say, I learned how all these procedures should be done. Before I could say I could really do them, one hell of a lot of practice would be necessary. But now, I at least knew I *could* do them.

"I have to keep reminding myself," Joe said to me after class on Thursday. "When I work with you, sometimes I feel amazed at how I have to guide you through everything — the least little detail."

"I warned you," I said.

"Yes, you did," Joe replied. "But let me finish, all right? Given the level of supervision you need, I'm even more amazed at how well you do *what* you do. You're slow, but when it's done, it's done beautifully. And you seem to never make the same mistake twice. I hope you *will* go home after school and practice. I think you can become quite a good restorer, actually." Then, he sat down with me, and listed the tools I would need to buy, and where I might find them. It took him two hours, and the information covered five sheets of legal-size note paper.

That winter was truly one of discontent. Most of it was spent in mortal combat with a nasty, vicious little turn-of-the-century cylinder box that never should have been born in the first place, let alone resuscitated. After two months, the only visible results were an escalating number of scratches and gouges on both the mechanism and my hands. I considered offering the thing to the Iranians: let them melt it down and cast it into bullets, in which form it would be both less offensive and less dangerous. But the notion of eventually being able to improve the condition of good-quality machines made me persevere. I worked till I was stuck, and then I ran up world-class phone bills, talking cross-country to Nancy or Joe, who patiently explained what I needed to do to reestablish control over my opponent. I singlehandedly supported the Washington State Ferry Commission that winter, taking pieces of my grubby little nemesis across the Sound to Port Orchard, where Bill Ullstrom, with unfailing good humor, would bail me out.

By the end of February, I had the job done, but I couldn't feel satisfied. "It sounds terrible," I told Bill.

"It sounds as good as it ever did," Bill said laconically. "That's because it's a garbage box. It's a late, production-line model, and it sounded terrible when it came out of the factory. Nothing you could do would make it sound good. I couldn't make it sound good. *Elton Norwood* couldn't make it sound good."

Elton Norwood, in Denver, was generally acclaimed at the time to be the premier restorer of cylinder music boxes in the country.

"Hide it in a closet," Bill continued. "Or sell it. Or pitch it into the wastebasket. Then, go fix another one. You did just fine. I think you've got the knack for this sort of work. You've just gotta keep at it."

Bill was not an effusive man; those were words of high praise indeed. I took the ferry back home, and tore right into a reasonably decent 11-inch cylinder box.

This time, the job went much better. Only a couple of calls to New York, and one ferry trip to Port Angeles, and six weeks later, I was the very proud owner of a nice, shiny machine that played clear and sweet. "I'm impressed," Myra said. "I really am. I've got to admit, I wondered if you could do it."

"Let the doubters cease their wonder," I said. "Mr. Fixit is on his way."

"You sure do know how to take a compliment, don't you?" said my wife.

"You know my motto," I said. "Horrible in defeat; obnoxious in victory."

The third box went even better; after finishing it, I took off for upstate New York for a week of graduate study with Nancy and Joe that I hoped would tighten up my loose ends and smooth my rough edges. Then, shortly after I returned home, I got just the break I needed. Another collector offered to sell me what he described as a nice interchangeable cylinder box. I had in fact been looking for a nice interchangeable cylinder box, so I asked him about the condition of the machine.

"It's good," he said. "Very good, in fact. It's got six cylinders, and it sits up on an attractive table. It's been all restored, and it works perfectly, except for one thing."

"Oh?" I said. "What might that be?"

"It needs damper work," said the collector. "There's a lot of damper noise. But that's it. I was going to do it myself, but I've had it for a couple of years now, and frankly, I don't think I'll ever get to it. So, I'd just as soon sell it."

Damper work is the *bête noire* of most music box restorers. The very earliest music boxes suffered from an abundance of unwanted, distracting noises which tended to irritate listeners to the point of spoiling the fine musical arrangements. Then, in 1815, Francois Nicole, in Geneva, determined that if he were to implant a tiny curved steel wire, very much like the hairspring of a watch, beneath the tip of a tooth, the advancing pins would push the wire against the tooth tip, thereby stopping any residual vibrations from a previous "hit" before the pin plucked the tooth again. Thus did Nicole banish the squeaks, grunts, and chirps from the music box, while simultaneously condemning his occupational descendants (and perhaps himself, as well) to endless bouts of dyspepsia, shaking palsy, and premature blindness.

"Well, okay," I said to my collector-acquaintance. "I guess I can give it a try. I know how to do dampers."

The music box turned out to be exactly as described, an attractive, shining machine that ran smoothly and properly. It was a good-quality box, manufactured in the 1890's by the Paillard Company, and it was unusual, perhaps even unique. Paillard had made a type of interchangeable-cylinder mechanism called the Gloria: to permit the safe removal and changing of the cylinders, a round, steel layshaft was placed beneath the bedplate, directly linking the spring to the governor, thereby taking the cylinder out of the power linkage. Paillard also manufactured a small number of an unusual noninterchangeable cylinder box known as a polytype: the cylinders of these machines played six tunes, and the cylinders were pinned so as to produce striking accompaniment effects which were different for each tune. According to the colorful card inside the lid, my box was a Gloria-Polytype, and a review of the music-box literature persuaded me that it just might be the only one of its kind in existence.

Now, I could tell by looking at the layshaft under the bedplate that my new acquisition was indeed a Gloria, but other than by the information on the card inside the lid, I could not have told that it was a polytype — nor, for that matter, could I have told much of anything about its music. I had never before heard such squeaking, squawking, groaning, and burping sounds from a music box. It sounded like a nature sanctuary, full of great hordes of birds, crickets, katydids, and frogs both little and large. It was difficult to hear the notes for the noises.

Myra looked dismayed. "I thought it was absolutely beautiful," she said. "Until you turned it on."

"Well, I can't say I wasn't warned," I said. "It's as described — exactly. So, now, I'll get to learn a lot about dampers, won't I?"

Somewhere, someone was laughing — and I'm not talking about the previous owner of the music box. Though I suppose it was likely that he too may have been enjoying a good chuckle.

I began my assault on the noisemakers by straightening the cylinder pins. Though tedious, this is not a difficult job. With the cut-off end of a hypodermic needle on a syringe, one examines each of the pins on the cylinder, bending straight those which are deflected to the side. Otherwise, these pins would strike the tooth tips off center, producing very nonmusical sounds — or, if bent very far, they might even pluck an adjacent tooth here and there, which would introduce wrong notes into the arrangements. A person can do this sort of work for only a couple of hours at a time before his neck goes into spasm and his hand begins to twitch convulsively. Thus, it takes a good week or so before an entire cylinder, with its five to seven thousand pins, is appropriately aligned for the comb teeth. But of course, I had six cylinders to do, not one, and there were a goodly number of bent pins on each. It was close to two months, then, before I could really check for the improvement in sound. And when I did, the answer was unequivocal. There was none.

So, I turned to the dampers, the tiny curved wires set into small, pinned recesses beneath the comb teeth. They must be placed just so, such that the pins will contact them and push them squarely against the undersides of the tooth tips immediately before the pin plucks the tooth. Without dampers, the pins might come into contact with a tooth while it was still vibrating from a previous "hit", and then the result would be a buzzing sound. Or, if the damper wire is too light or too heavy, or if it is not pushed cleanly and evenly against the tooth, it will produce one of a seemingly-infinite number of unpleasant, distracting noises. Using a set of tiny tools, some of them made specifically for this purpose, the restorer first removes the holding pin along with the old damper wire or fragment thereof, cleans out the hole, inserts the new wire, fixes the holding pin back into place, and then shapes the wire to proper form.

I removed the combs, and set to work. It was slow, but I was making noticeable progress. After about a week, I found myself approaching the middle of the comb, and I told myself I'd do one more damper before I quit for the night. But then as I pulled the pin, I felt, more than heard, a snap. Looking more closely, I saw I had broken the tip off the end of the tooth.

I felt dizzy; I thought I might actually throw up. A perfect comb, and on a valuable, classic music box. I felt as if I had wrenched the leg off a newborn baby as I was delivering it. That night was not one for sleeping, and early the next morning, I called Nancy in upstate New York. Her reaction was to wonder in astonishment at what I was moaning about. "You knocked out a tip?" she said. "Big deal! How about if I tell you that once, I accidentally knocked a comb I was carrying against the side of a vise, and I knocked out the three bass teeth? There they went — bouncing and clattering all over the floor."

"God, what did you *do*?" I said.

"What do you think I did?" she retorted. "I wasn't about to throw out the music box. I just sat down and put new teeth back in, so it looked as good as new. Just like you're going to sit back down and put that tip back in. Good grief, Larry, *everybody* does shit like that. If you're going to work at fixing things, sometimes you're going to make something worse. But only temporarily. Come on, now; shape up. This is a good education for you."

I went back to the workshop, put a new tip into the damaged tooth, and continued — with a vastly increased level of respect for the always-lurking dark forces of destruction — to complete the row of dampers. Then, I screwed the combs back into place on the bedplate. The good news was that now I had in fact made a difference. The bad news was that the music sounded *worse*. It actually did. It was as if every one of those sanctuary critters had bred a family during the couple of weeks I was down in my workshop with the combs. Concerto for Squeak and Groan. It was hideous.

Now, this was as discouraging as it was puzzling, and I was forced to give up on the notion of having the music box ready to play for my visitors at that year's Annual Musical Box Society Convention. Still, I made certain to ask my friend Angelo Rulli, from St. Paul, to take a look at the thing. Which Angelo did. He frowned as he peered underneath the comb, and then, as the instrument began to play, he rubbed his chin as if to assuage his pain. Finally, as tactfully as he could — for Angelo is as kind a man as he is honest — he showed me that the curves in my dampers were far too flat. "Look," Angelo said, as we peered like goggle-eyed twins through our jeweler's loupes. "When the pin comes close, instead of just nudging the very end of the damper against the tip of the tooth, it actually catches the damper between itself and the tooth. So you can't help but get a noise." Then, Angelo went on to tell me that he thought I was making a serious error in trying to do the work myself. "This is a museum piece," he said. "It really is. What you ought to be doing is practicing on smaller boxes until you're really good. I mean, *really* good. Give this one to one of the pros before you snap off any more of its teeth."

When a man sets out in kindness to help his friend, he will always succeed — though perhaps not precisely in the manner he intended. For a couple of months, I didn't touch Gloria, as I pondered Angelo's advice. But I didn't simply sit and mull. I read — everything I could get my hands on about dampering. I tried a few practice swipes at shaping dampers on a small comb from a non-descript, less-than-ordinary music box. And in so doing, I brought myself to a decision. Any way I considered it, working on garbage boxes was a meaningless activity –- just something to get done and over with ASAP. There was no interest, no satisfaction. The only way I was going to improve my skills was to work on machines that reached out from within their cases, grabbed me by my shirt collar, and shook me hard. And besides: when considered from the dampering point of view, Gloria's combs were no different from those of junker-boxes. The teeth were wide, and there was considerable space between them. True, many of the fine early key-wound boxes had teeth as narrow as needles, one right on top of the other, and the dampers were so anchored that they needed to be drilled out. No way I should be working on one of those boxes . . . not yet. There was only one way, though, that I'd get good enough to ever work on them, and that road led directly through Gloria. Besides, she was so noisy. There had to be something important to learn here.

Once again, somebody somewhere laughed. But this time, I heard sympathy, rather than derision, in the mirth. I unscrewed Gloria's combs, and went back down to my work shop.

Thus began a truly extraordinary experience, a titanic tug-of-war between man and machine that was to occupy close to a year of my attention. I made my dampers more round, and then flattened them just a bit again. I curved them closer to the tips of the teeth, and then farther back toward the roots. I tried heavier, and then lighter, wires. I brought the tips of the dampers closer to the tips of the teeth, and then moved them farther away. And each maneuver I attempted, of course, I had to test — and there was only one way to do that. Through equal parts of trial and error, I learned that the most consistent musical passage for evaluation was the middle portion of *The Star Spangled Banner*, where the birds and the frogs sang a striking countermelody to the rockets' red glare and the bombs bursting in air. And each audition gave clear proof, through the months, that I was not near-ly there.

"My God," Myra said one night. "I don't see how you can stand taking that comb off, putting it on again, and then having to take it right off again." Though her major tone was one of desperation, I thought I could also pick up on just a hint of admiration. Unless that was just wishful thinking.

"I don't know of any other way to go about it," I said. "And besides, look at all I'm learning."

"Like *what*?" said my spouse.

"Like everything that won't work," I answered, and, with the comb, disappeared quickly down the stairs to the work shop.

After a while, I noticed that I'd gotten rid of a great deal of the noise, but there remained some amazingly loud and consistent sounds, primarily traceable to six or eight specific comb teeth. I began to wonder whether this problem could be something other than dampers. I extended my range of reading; I began to call Nancy and other friends who were experienced restorers. Could it be registration? If the comb was not lined up precisely with the cylinder, the pins would strike the teeth — and the dampers — off center, and produce noises. But a careful check revealed this to not be the case: the tips of the teeth were perfectly aligned with the cylinder pins. And when I altered the setting of the small metal registration peg at the end of the cylinder, such that the cylinder was shifted first to the left a bit, and then to the right, the music box responded by broadcasting noises that could have sent flocks of gaily-plumaged birds flapping hysterically for cover deep in a grove of banyan trees. No, registration was not the problem.

Were the tips of the teeth worn irregularly, from long, hard use, so that contact between them and the pins was erratic? Or were the pins worn irregularly? A careful check with a high-powered magnifier indicated that such was not the case.

How about the pin-tip relationship? Considering the angle of inclination of the comb, were the pins set (and straightened) in the cylinder at the proper angle, such that they would pluck the teeth cleanly, and not slide off one side of the tooth or the other? A couple of hours of close observation confirmed that no adjustment of any sort was required in this regard.

My, I had learned a lot! But the box still sounded awful, and I had run out of ideas. It was time for the Ultimate Weapon. I picked up the phone, and called Joe Ira.

At the time of my call, Joe was eighty-three years old. His idea of a happy day, and time well spent, was ten, twelve, or fourteen hours at his cellar workbench, restoring a basket case of a clock or a music box to perfect health. His hand was steady enough to place and shape dampers without the aid of magnification — sometimes without even looking at the comb, while he was explaining the procedure to a goggling tyro. Joe told me that he couldn't promise anything, but sure, bring the box down, and he'd have a look at it with me.

As I carried the machine into his house, Joe seemed impressed. "Oh, that's a beauty," he said. "It ought to sound fantastic."

He liked my music box: this was a good start. "It ought to, all right," I replied, as I wrestled it down the stairs to the cellar. "Let's see what you can make of it."

"Joe looked, and then he listened. "Oh, it's got to be the dampers," he said. "It's just gotta be."

"I think so too, Joe," I said. "But I just can't think of anything else to try with them."

He pointed at my magic-marker dots near the roots of seven teeth. "These seem to be the bad ones?" he said.

I nodded.

"Okay. Let's see."

He took off the comb, and then peered at the undersides of the teeth. After a minute or two — no more — his scowl of concentration gave way to a small grin, at once knowing and mischievous. A lovely sight on the face of a man in his mid-eighties. "Let's try something," Joe muttered. He took up his damper-shaping tweezers, and for perhaps three minutes, he fiddled with the dampers on the marked teeth. Then, he passed the comb to me, up over his right shoulder. "Here," he said. "Take a look."

I looked, but I didn't know what to say. The dampers in question were now altered so that their tips were not only set relatively far back along the tooth tips, but were separated from the teeth by an astonishingly wide gap. Joe rescued me by saying, "Looks sort of funny, doesn't it?"

I allowed that it did. I allowed, in fact, that I'd never seen a damper even remotely resembling these.

"No," Joe said. "You won't. I've never seen it in any book, and I've never seen any other restorer do it this way. That gap's roughly thirty thousandths, and nobody else sets them at more than ten. But every so often, I come across one of these very noisy boxes, and this little trick seems to work for me. Let's put the comb back on, and see how it sounds."

For the first time in my hearing, the rockets glared and the bombs burst, almost completely free of the interfering noises of the creatures of the night. I must have had a very funny look on my face, because Joe looked highly amused. "*Why*, Joe?" I said. "*How?*"

"I'm not sure," Joe answered. "I'm really not. But here — look underneath while the thing is playing. You can see how the pin just does pick that damper up, and then just barely touches the end of it to the tooth, without either catching it and pinching it, or making it scrape backwards. It *works*. So I use it."

I was amazed, but I asked myself why I should be. How many times had I told a patient that a particular medication seemed to cure or ameliorate a disease, but that we didn't have the faintest clue as to just how? "It *works*," I had so often said. "So we use it."

"Take it home, now," Joe told me. "It's still got a few noises. Do what I did on some of those other teeth. Then, it'll sound perfect."

I did and it did. Less than five hours of work later, I played through the entire program on the six cylinders, and not a sound other than the music could be heard. I could make out the polytype arrangements: there was a very effective tremolo section toward the middle of *Home Sweet Home*, and a parade of bright, cheerful piccolo notes did much to enhance the *Liberty Bell March*. As deep as the frustrations had run over the past year, the satisfaction of this moment ran deeper. And as I was taking my proper pride and pleasure in the clear, splendid musical arrangements, I realized that I was also listening to a voice emanating from somewhere within the music itself. "This is how it *should* sound," the voice said. "It was good that you didn't give up. "

But why? I thought. How *did* that crazy dampering work?

"Look at the box," I heard. "Look closely. And then, the next time you find another music box like this — and you will — don't throw up your hands and run away. Play it. Watch it play. Play with it. Take all the time you need. Don't ever think of any music box you've worked on as being finished, not ever. Because there are so many ways to make the music sound better — and you will never find them all. Neither the music nor you will ever be perfect."

I've heard a few other noisy boxes by now, but I've not been able to make any of them sound as good as my Gloria Polytype still does, let alone figure out the cause or causes of this odd condition. But I tell myself that maybe the next box will drop the clue, and I wait for it with an odd sort of anticipation, blended, it seems, of roughly equal parts of hope and fear.

Meanwhile, I've graduated to work on some high-quality key-winds, those marvelous early cylinder boxes with needle-tipped teeth packed sardine-style the length of the cylinder. I've replaced their tiny dampers; I've drilled out inaccessible pins. I've registered cylinders. I've taken the tuning of combs, and, where necessary, adjusted the tuning of individual teeth. I've fiddled with comb inclination angles, and moved comb settings backwards and forward, learning in the process how a revision of as little as one-thousandth of an inch can make a major alteration (for better or worse) in the quality of the music. Once, as I was fussing over a lovely little key-wind, made around 1840 by the superb craftsman Reymond-Nicole, I noticed that moving the comb ever so slightly backward while making the most minuscule adjustment toward the left suddenly eliminated a mildly unpleasant twanging quality, and a vague "mushy" disclarity. The music became suddenly exquisite in its precision, with well-timed chord sequences in the bass punctuating long, running single-note treble passages, the whole moving in and out of minor modes, piling up one unresolved statement on another, to seemingly bypass the ear and deliver a musical appeal directly to the heart of the listener. The minimal, delicate comb adjustment gave voice to a flow of emotions previously unsuspected and unrecognized. There was sadness; there was joy. Anxiety alternated with confidence; doubt finally gave way to affirmation. And through the entire program, there was the voice of the maker, searching, unrelentingly yearning, as clear today as it was roughly one hundred and fifty years ago, when the maker pinned his cylinder and painstakingly aligned the comb. "There's more yet that I need to tell you," he says. "Listen again. Don't stop listening."

So, as I restore, I listen; as I listen, I restore. And what I hear is more than notes of music, much more than the alternating compressions and rarefactions of air produced by the vibration of tuned tongues of steel being plucked by small, round steel pins. I hear Nancy's voice, and those of the two Restoring Joes. I hear my dear friend, Angelo. I encourage them to feel at home in my shop, because not only do I enjoy their company, but so often in their running conversations and commentary, I'll pick up just the suggestion I need to break free of an obstruction in my current restoration project. Frequently, the problem is not that I don't know how to do the thing; it's a matter of an inappropriate point of view. I look, but I don't see. But as I shift my angle of observation, and try to consider the situation through Nancy's eyes, say, or Angelo's, the pieces fall into place, and then, the approach often becomes clear. So that when I talk to my friends by phone now, it's less often to ask them how to do something than to tell them how it went.

I hear the voices of the makers, as well. As I work over the boxes, listening to the progressive changes in the music as I go along, I hear the pot of emotions behind the notes, now, simmering gently, now raging to a boil. And in the finest boxes, there is always that tone of searching. Always seeking; always questioning. How can I adjust the comb to sharpen the focus? How can I adjust my innermost ear? While the music is playing, I can, at times, see the man who set it onto the cylinder and the comb. I can see the lines in his face, the pain and the joy in his eyes. Sometimes, his hands are stretched out before him: What does he want from me? What is he trying to say?

I keep listening. The more I listen, the more I hear, and the more compelling become the voices. And the fainter becomes the distinction between my work shop and my collection room. Sometimes, as I'm listening, I find myself thinking of a statue I saw recently in a town square. This monument to a man dead now fewer years than I have lived is already as lifeless as its prototype. Pigeon droppings run down its face and shirtfront; boys use it for target practice in their stone-throwing contests. Both the name and the grand title on the discolored plaque on the base have altogether lost their resonance.

In the sharpest contrast to this stands one of my smaller music boxes. This machine plays six dance tunes, none of which I can identify. And there are no identifying maker's marks — no clue whatever as to the identity of the person who conceived and delivered this little personal monument. Although the box was built some 150 years ago, its voice is still powerful, stirring and haunting. Every bar of the elegantly-arranged dance music pours out a tumult of the maker's feelings, such that in the most complex passages the listener has to contend with the impulse to cry out, "Yes, I hear you. I'm listening. Go on!" It occurred to me that Nabokov would have loved this box –- either that, or he would have envied it. It has the sound of a pure voice, of disembodied speech. The speaker completely effaced. The man become his message.

When the box came to me, it would not play at all, and as I worked on it, the progressive improvement in its voice both sustained me and drove me on. But finally I reached the limits of my capabilities, so I sent the box on to David Wells, an outstanding professional restorer, and a close friend. Whether the box sounds as good (or, perhaps, even better) now than it did when it was made is neither knowable nor important. Nor is it important that David could have done the part of the work I did more quickly, and probably even better. What matters is that having done what I did, so slowly and so carefully, I was in the process able to become acquainted with the maker — whoever he may have been — such that when I now listen to the box, I can hear his voice far more clearly than I possibly could have if I'd simply purchased the machine fully restored. And in addition, every now and again, I can hear my own voice joined with both the maker's and David's — though, as in any well-set-up chorus, I have difficulty telling where one voice leaves off and the others begin. Not that I try terribly hard. That's not important, either.

Neither does it seem important to concern myself any longer with the distinction between mental processes and manual labor. "Between the conception and the creation," Eliot wrote, "lies the shadow." Minds isolated from hands are as crippled as hands without minds. The line between thinking and doing is as arbitrary, and as dangerous in the limitations it imposes, as the line between my collection room and my work shop. It is a shadow line, and it vanishes altogether when viewed in light directed upon it from the proper angle.

An Organ for Expression

 have suffered my life long from a condition known as *cacoëthes scribendi.* Translated, this is an irresistible itch to write. Scribble, scribble.

Now, words mean more than they say straight out, which is the reason I chose to make my confession in Latin. Why, in the ancient Italian, the situation even *sounds* like a disease, doesn't it? Much more than just a nasty habit, not at all like picking one's nose, or chomping on fingernails. Not my fault. I can't help it any more than a diabetic can help having a high level of sugar in his blood. If I don't produce a decent number of words for a few days running, I become cranky and irritable. Once, when I mentioned that to my wife, she told me I sounded like an Ex-Lax commercial. Which didn't bother me, not really. Writers are supposed to suffer, aren't they?

Well, I've been writing and suffering for a long time. As a kid in grammar school, I'd make up stories about my classmates, or the animals who lived in the field back of school. Nothing really wrong with that, I guess, except that I'd be doing it while the teacher was explaining the essentials of long division, and then when it came time to do the arithmetic homework, I'd be lost at sea.

Of course, I never told either my parents or my teachers just why it was that I couldn't seem to learn my numbers. I had more sense than to do that. Today, such a kid would be proclaimed gifted (whatever might be the quality of his stories), channeled into special education, and mightily oohed and aahed over. Forty years ago, however, the only thing I would have been proclaimed was delinquent, and never mind whether my stories might have induced Saul Bellow to put down his pen in despair and consign Augie March to the wastebasket. The special education *I'd* have gotten would definitely not have been designed toward the improvement of my verbal and imaginative skills. I knew it was better to just let them all think I was dumb at math.

In high school, there was more suffering. From freshman year to graduation, the key feature of English class was the weekly theme. For every other kid, this was the bane of existence, the very blackest of pits. For me, it was heaven. Drew Pearson never had it so good. A regular column, with a guaranteed readership. My only problem was managing to keep it down to just one measly paper a week. One a *day* would have been more like it. Not only did I hand in my weekly ruminations on time, I also invariably came away with an A, and this did not exactly make me eligible for the Most Popular Boy Award. The names my classmates stuck on me make me blush even thirty years in retrospect. And I didn't dare let anyone know I actually *liked* writing those papers. They'd have hung me from the nearest sour apple tree.

This pattern continued into college. Freshman English, weekly themes. My roommate, a member of the college wrestling team, began to grouse that the professor marked papers automatically. "Whatever *you* write, he puts down an A," he complained. "Whatever *I* write, it's a C-minus. I bet if I handed in your paper next week, and you handed in mine, you'd still get your A, and I'd still get a C-minus."

No one's ego is immaculate, utterly free of touchy spots. There was no way in the world I was going to let the English professor read a paper written by my roommate, and think I was the author. "Tell you what," I said. "You wouldn't let me stand in for you at a wrestling match, would you? Well, that's the way I feel about my papers. Nobody's going to write one for *me*. But if you want, I'll write yours for you. How's that?"

My roommate blinked. "You're gonna write your paper *and* mine?" he said. "*Two* papers in one week? And I don't have to write *any*?"

I knew that was an offer he'd never be able to refuse. I wrote his paper and mine, typed them both up, and we handed them in.

And sure enough, a few days later, back came my A and his C-minus."

"I told you so!" he crowed.

It wasn't a fair experiment, but my roommate still doesn't know that. I'd read most of his previous efforts, and it was no trouble at all to turn out a paper that could easily have come from his very own pen. That English professor was one sharp cookie, a former Navy officer with a bear-trap mind and a razor blade for a tongue. Had I written my roommate's paper as if it were mine, the prof would have picked it up in a second. So, what I'd really shown was that I could write a tricky piece well enough to take in a highly critical reader. It was a heady thought. But this definitely was going to remain my secret. "Yup," I replied to my indignant roommate. "You were right." Then, I listened and commiserated as he bewailed the unfairness of the world. Which was fine. A few of his complaints came in handy later in the term, when we had to write on the question, "Is God Dead or Alive?"

During medical school, internship, and residency, I was too busy to do more than take a scattering of notes here and there on my more interesting and peculiar patients and colleagues. But then, when my bewhiskered uncle insisted on supporting me for a couple of years so that I could deliver Navy brats in Rhode Island, I decided to try my hand at some short stories. And for the first time, I found myself dissatisfied with something I'd written. The stories seemed both flat and derivative to me, and editors from *The Atlantic* to the Pacific were unanimous in their endorsement of that judgement.

So, I let the old world take a couple of turns, and then, back in civilian life and a member of the faculty at the University of Washington School of Medicine, I set out to work my medical training notes into a book. At the same time, it occurred to me that I was writing a considerable number of magazine articles about genetic engineering; this was during the early 1970's, when, to read the paper, a person could easily conclude that gene transfusions, clones, and made-to-order babies were right around the corner. No reason why *this* stuff couldn't be developed into a book, too, I thought. So, I developed it. And, *mirabile dictu*, both books were published. True, both made every Worst Seller List in existence, but that didn't discourage me. I'd enjoyed writing them, and I thought they were good. And I was young. It was a beginning. But a beginning to what, I had no idea.

What it was, I soon discovered, was a beginning to *real* suffering. Ten years in the inferno, you might call it. I tried a science-fiction novel; it stank. I wrote three full-length novels: I thought they all stank. In response to my family and friends, who insisted that I was much too harsh a judge, I submitted each of the novels to publishers. And each editor agreed that basically, yes, the books did stink. Oh, they *were* well written, no question about that. But there was no narrative drive. No color. They just plodded along. They were not page-turners.

Which actually surprised me not at all. For some time, I'd been aware that I was having a great deal of difficulty in satisfactorily transferring my thoughts to paper. A verbal idea that sent waves of the most gorgeous song vibrating through my brain would lie on a piece of paper like a dead flounder. Talk about loss in translation! The sad monochrome letters on the page never seemed to bear more than a superficial resemblance to the rich, textured mental image from which they sprang.

I sank ever more deeply into frustration. I snorted when I heard it said that writers have only one story to tell, and I shuddered when I read that John Cheever told, basically, the same story over and over again, feeling that he had never got it quite right. I wondered about writers like Margaret Mitchell. Had she gotten GWTW perfect the first time, and then been left with nothing more to say? Or had she simply decided that writing was a mug's game, and given up in disgust?

Then, I began to notice something else. It seemed to me that even the best writers — or, at least, the writers *I* liked best — were incapable of producing a communication nearly as forceful, or as powerful, or as compelling, as that of a musical composer. Saul Bellow's play of ideas was mightily impressive, as were Stanley Elkin's verbal pyrotechnics. Philip Roth made me chuckle and gasp, and Bernard Malamud's Jews and Cheever's WASPS invariably left me in a well-crafted mood of bittersweet nostalgia. But compared to music, it was all pretty weak stuff. No writer — no religious leader, even — has given voice to affirmation with anything like the power of Brahms, in his First Symphony. Beethoven's

Ninth does the same thing for a vision of celestial glory, and with all due respect to Schiller, one need not understand a single word of *Ode to Joy* in order to comprehend this vision to the fullest. The exuberance of youth in springtime is a favorite topic of novels, but the nineteen-year-old Bizet said it all (and said it better) in his First (and only) Symphony. And who has ever put into words the feeling for his country that comes through in Smetana's *Ma Vlast?*

One could go on and on (And one sometimes does). This evocative power of music is not limited to the classics — not at all. Just last evening, my wife and I were listening to a recording of ragtime music. One of the tunes was *Eli Green's Cakewalk*, a snappy, delightful little piece by Sadie Koninsky. All of a sudden, I was in a green park, staring at a brass band and a pianist up on an octagonal bandstand. It was a summer Sunday afternoon — July, I thought, with the temperature up into the eighties — and the men in their derbies, striped shirts, and red suspenders were walking arm-in-arm with ladies in long dresses and floppy, beflowered hats. Some couples had spread picnics on the grass. An occasional ice-cream vendor was roaming around, doing a good business. A young woman walked slowly up to the bandstand, paused for a moment, and then climbed the stairs, lifting the hem of her dress before her so as to not step on it. She walked up to the piano player, a young black man with a round face. Continuing to pound the rhythm with his left hand, he looked up and gave her a wide smile. What was that she was saying to him, leaning over from the waist so he could hear her above the music? She wanted to sing with the band; would he mind that? The pianist's smile faded; he glanced out into the crowd. Would he *mind?* Well, it wasn't exactly a matter of would he mind, but this gal was white, and the whole damn band was black. And looky there, down below, look at those three men pointing and whispering already, and making ugly faces, just because the gal was up there. If she started to sing, those guys were probably gonna do a hell of a lot more than point and whisper.

At that point, my wife said something; I still don't know what. I blinked my way back to her. Later, I tried to recapture that world and those people, but I couldn't. I tried and tried. I even played the record again, but it was no go. What had *happened* to those people, and that world? I'd been right there, right smack in the middle of them; where had they gone? I sat down at the typewriter, and tried to write the scene back into existence, but once again it was a case of polychrome in the head and monochrome on paper. I could no more describe the thicket of emotions at the heart of that musical image than I could put into words Brahms' affirmation, Beethoven's vision of celestial glory, Bizet's springtime exuberance, or Smetana's patriotism. I seemed to be floating helplessly somewhere between perception and expression. Between the languages of music and words there is a gap, and that gap felt unbridgeable. At least by me.

To say the least, this was discouraging. To have talent but no ambition is sad; to have ambition but no talent even worse. But to have the wrong talent to serve your particular ambition may be the worst situation of all.

Well, why not just cross over? Try writing some music. Maybe that would get my ideas across to my satisfaction.   Because I'm a musical illiterate. I don't know tuning from temperament. Scales are an utter mystery. I can't tell a major third from a minor fifth. I should write music? Impossible. I don't know nuthin'.

A person has to start somewhere.

I don't even know where to start.

Scribble, scribble.

But you have to stay open to possibilities.

I read the classified ads in the newspapers, looking for old music boxes and phonographs. Admittedly, this is not a terribly productive source: usually, the machines are nothing special, or the advertisers want more money than I'm willing to spend. Or both.

Every so often, though . . .

I noticed an ad: CLOCK ORGAN, it said, followed by a phone number. That was all. This had to be followed up. Some seventeenth- and eighteenth-century clocks were fitted with small (20 to 40-note) pipe organs, which were set up so that the music would play on the hour. These instruments came to be called flute organs, due to the quality of their tone, and they are no less prized by collectors today than they were by their original owners, who were usually members of the royalty or the high nobility. Most important, the barrels of some flute organs are pinned with music composed specifically for that instrument by Handel, Haydn or Mozart. In fact, it has been discovered that some works by these composers have survived only on the particular machines for which they were written.

Now, fine old clock organs are not frequently or easily found, and to say the least, it's terribly unlikely that one is going to turn up in a want ad in the *Seattle Times*. But odd things do happen. So, I called.

A woman answered the phone. Well, she told me, she didn't have the organ in her home; it was in her father's house, and he lived down in Tacoma, and why didn't I give him a call . . .

I was close — mighty close — to saying thank you, and hanging up. Lots of want ads turn out to be odd people, doing something strange, or peculiar, or even downright unpleasant. This situation had the ring of a first-class family squabble. Maybe Dad really did want to sell the organ, but maybe he didn't. Maybe this sister wanted him to sell, but another sister wanted him to keep it and leave it to her in his will. Or, maybe the organ didn't even belong to a Dad at all; maybe it had been liberated by the caller from the home of some wealthy collector in Southern California. But then, the woman mentioned that her father's name was Roy.

Suddenly, the entire situation changed. Organ, Tacoma, Roy. "His name isn't Roy *Norman,* is it?" I asked.

"Why, yes," said the woman. "How did *you* know?"

It wasn't exactly a case for Sherlock Holmes. Anyone in mechanical music circles in the Pacific Northwest knows that Roy Norman, in Tacoma, has been playing with, collecting, restoring, and building mechanical organs for more years than many of us have been on the earth. For example, Roy put together a small band organ for each of his grandchildren. Put each one together from scratch, that is. Not from kits. From plain pieces of wood, and metal, and leather. From scratch.

"I'm in the Musical Box Society," I said, and I mentioned my name.

"Oh!" The woman's voice brightened. "Well, that's fine. I'm sure he'll be glad to hear from you. He had a car accident recently —"

"Is he all right?" I asked.

"Oh, yes. He's still getting some physical therapy, but he's okay. But it did show him that he really should not be driving any more, so he's moving into a retirement community. We're helping him clean out the house. Go ahead; give him a call. Here's his number."

I paused for a moment after I hung up. Roy hadn't been active in the Society for the past four or five years; after his wife had died, he'd slowed down greatly in all his activities. Now, he was leaving his long-time home, making that move that all older people know is their next to last. Did I really want to be a cog in Roy's misery machine?

But an overly sensitive collector can't expect to have very much of a collection. Any time a really good antique or collectible becomes available, you can bet there's a pretty depressing reason for it.

And besides, Roy's daughter knew my name. Suppose she told Roy I was going to call him, and I never did?

Roy didn't sound good when he answered the phone. His answers were short and gruff. I wondered whether he might be having trouble breathing. Yes, he said, he remembered me, all right, and yes, he really *was* OK. But it was time to move; he just couldn't get along in the house by himself any more. And the machine he had for sale was indeed an old organ from a clock, a nice one, he thought. He hadn't finished working on it, but he'd made it a whole set of new pipes, and a new barrel.

"A new . . . *barrel*?" I said.

"Yeah. Couldn't get the old one to play. So I made a new one. Got *Music Box Dancer* on it."

All of a sudden, I wasn't interested in the organ. I knew that if Roy had done the work, it would be superb. But *Music Box Dancer* on an eighteenth-century organ which once might have played airs by Haydn or Mozart? No, that just wouldn't do. Again, I might have said thank you, and hung up, but this wasn't a faceless voice at the other end of a phone line. You don't simply cut off an old acquaintance at a bad time of his life because you don't particularly want to buy the organ he has for sale. Thinking what I might say next, I asked, "Do you have any other organs you want to sell, Roy?"

"Yeah. Got a 63-keyless Ruth band organ copy. Built it myself. Almost finished. Want to sell it, too. It's a good one."

I was sure it was, but a band organ was just about the last thing I was interested in buying. These huge machines are the kind that provide music for merry-go-rounds; the ones that can send small children flying across the arcade at the first blast from their raucous, shrieking pipes. Kept indoors, they can easily shatter glass, plaster walls, and eardrums. As if I had room in my house to put one, anyway.

"Want to come and see it?" Roy continued. "I'll be at the house all day tomorrow. Whyn't you come on by?"

"Sure, Roy," I said. "I'll be glad to. See you tomorrow."

When I told Myra about the anachronistic flute organ, she cringed; when I mentioned the band organ, she looked at me as though I had announced my intention of flapping my arms and taking off for Mars. "You *can't* be serious," she said, in that spousespeak tone that implies command, rather than questioning.

"Oh, of course not; no," I said. "But what else could I say? *Or* do? Would *you* have told Roy to just forget it; that you didn't want to go over there and see his machines. And him, too, just by the way?"

She sighed, the wifely sound of necessary, if unwilling, capitulation. "No, I couldn't have done that," she said. "But it just makes me nervous. I know you."

"Come on," I said. "A flute organ with *Music Box Dancer* and a giant band organ. How much less likely could it be?"

She rolled her eyes. "I *know* you," she repeated. "The less likely it seems, the more likely it is."

Roy greeted us cheerfully the next day, and then introduced us to his two daughters and their husbands, who were helping him clean out the house. It appeared that they were nearly done. The living room, the hallway, and the kitchen were almost empty. Roy pulled at my sleeve. "Lemme take you down, and show you that organ," he said.

Myra stayed up with the daughters as I followed him down the stairs into the basement. Roy moved slowly. He seemed to have difficulty turning his neck, and his knees didn't bend very readily. He kept a firm grip on the handrail. But everything considered, he didn't look bad. His face had good color, and his eyes were clear and alert.

At the bottom of the steps, he turned left, raised his arm slowly, and gestured. "There she is," he said.

I swallowed. This was not going to be easy to get out of. The organ was massive. It was more than six feet tall, and almost six feet wide — a size to match its sound. Here was a machine suited for a person with a big barn to display it in, and with the inclination and the facilities to load it every now and again on to a trailer and haul it a thousand miles or more to join with fifty or more like-minded fanatics in an organ rally. Don't misunderstand: there was nothing wrong with the machine, not at all. Just try to imagine a shut-in trying to keep a St. Bernard in an 800-square-foot apartment.

Band organs are big in all respects. They originated in the late nineteenth century as a sort of hybrid, one side of their parentage being the famous (some would say infamous) organ-grinder's barrel organ, and the other being the old European barrel orchestrion, a giant machine founded upon an upright piano, with xylophones, drums, bells, wood blocks, and other raucous noisemakers as accompaniment. The earlier band organs played from either perforated paper rolls or "books" consisting of folded perforated squares of heavy cardboard. The music strip passed across a steel bar rather like the tracker bar of a player piano: where a perforation occurred, a spring-loaded lever (called a key) would pop up, permitting a valve beneath to open so that air would flow through and sound the corresponding organ reed. The key would remain open and sounding as long as the perforation lasted. Later, the pneumatic apparatus of the player piano was more directly applied, so that when a perforation passed over a hole in the band organ's tracker bar, the suction in the chamber beneath was released, and the proper valve would spring open. Thus, with the levers eliminated, these organs were called keyless, and so, in the jargon of the faithful, Roy's creation was a 63-keyless Ruth-copy band organ. And as large as it was, it was not nearly as big as they come. Organs as large as 96-keyless are not uncommon, and there exist some superdreadnoughts of as many as 112, or even 140 keys.

Roy ran his hand lightly along the left side of the case. "I built a lotta organs," he said. "One for all five of my grandchildren, and plenty more besides. This's my last one, and it's my biggest, too." He paused a moment, and then laughed, a real old-man's cackle. "Also, my best."

I came closer to get a better look. Though by no stretch of anyone's imagination could I be called knowledgable about band organs, this one looked close to being completed. It had no decorative facade, but the case was full and intact, and all the pipes appeared to be present. My situation was growing more desperate by the moment. This labor of love was a work of art. The pipes, all handcrafted from seasoned spruce, were perfectly proportioned, attractively varnished, and set carefully into place so as to be certain to please the eye as well as the ear. Pipes representing different voices — violins, flutes, ocarinas (yes, that's right), trumpets — were arranged, choir-like, so that the longest pipes of each rank were at the center, and the tallest ranks of pipes stood toward the rear. Farthest back, on either side, sat the eight trombone pipes, the deepest-voiced of them so long that they had to undergo two ninety-degree turns to accommodate to the spatial restrictions of the case.

"Can't see the bass pipes," Roy said. "They're on the underside, underneath the bottom panel."

A rear view of the machine permitted an appreciation of the operating mechanism, revealing the electric motor attached to the drive-wheel pulley; through this linkage, both the air supply and the music-strip drive would be operated. Roy pointed proudly at the neat, trim bellows. "Best bellows-cloth you can buy," he said. Then, he showed me the individual note-playing air pouches, linked below to the bellows and above, by a spaghetti-like mass of black, rubber tubing, to the tracker-bar and therefore to the music. "Can't get better pouch-leather than that, either," he said. "All the finest materials. That's all I put into this organ."

I saw a length of clear, plastic tubing, attached at one end to the bellows, but loose at the the other end. "Roy, where's this supposed to be attached?" I said.

He stared for a few seconds, and then shook his head. "Dunno," he said. "Can't remember."

I tried to say something, but I couldn't get the words past my throat. I remembered a passage from *The Boys of Summer*, in which Roger Kahn, walking with the soon-to-die Jackie Robinson on a cold day in New York was shocked at the awareness that he — Kahn — was slowing his own pace so that he would not be walking too rapidly for Jackie Robinson. Roy Norman couldn't remember where a hose on an organ should be attached. That was unthinkable.

"Well, okay, Roy," I finally managed to say. "We'll take a look and figure it out later." As I spoke, I realized I was also asking myself where in hell I was going to put this machine, and quickly gave myself a stern reprimand.

"Uh-huh," Roy said. "Well, lemme get an extension cord, and I'll try and play it for you."

He finally found the cord, plugged the organ in, and set a short music strip into place. However, the registration system had not been fully constructed and attached to the machine, so the proper instructions could not be sent via the pneumatic channels as to which groups of pipes should and should not be playing. Consequently, what came through was more gibberish than music. But although the notes made no melodic sense, the tone was clear and stunning. Full-throated laughter ran through every passage. Clearly, something was amusing this machine. It rolled its eyes as it spoke, and smiled mischievously; every now and again, it would wink in my direction. The temporary lack of musical message seemed unimportant: I knew that registration would take care of that, and in short order. Far more significant was the organ's voice. It left me with the distorted, disorienting sense that I was staring into some sort of carnival mirror of sound. The voice that organ was speaking in was mine.

A few words about voice — specifically, writer's voice. This is often confused with style, but the two are very different. Over the phone, or with your back turned, you can usually tell whether Uncle Charley is speaking to you, or whether it's Uncle Nate, and this has nothing to do with what's actually being said. To go a step further, the writer John Irving speaks to us in a deeply earnest voice, but Joseph Heller comes across as mocking and irreverent. Yet, both authors manage to convey a strong sense of indignation at the state of the world. Content aside, Henry Miller — speaking as the ultimate scamp — could not possibly be confused with digni-fied, proper Henry James. And anyone at all acquainted with the literature of the past twenty years would have little trouble deciding whether a particular paragraph had been written by Saul Bellow, Bernard Malamud, or Philip Roth.

A writer's voice is an integral part of his identity, and for better and worse, he's stuck with what he's got. Just as an attempt by a speaker to sound like Chauncey Depew or F. D. R. will inevitably render him ineffective, so will a writer fall on his face if he tries to make himself sound like Melville or Twain. A person's voice is as unique as his fingerprint. The magpie might wish to sound like the lion, but try as he might, he never will. At best he'll waste his time. At worst he'll destroy his vocal cords, and be forever after mute.

I was more than a little surprised to hear my own voice coming through the pipes of that band organ; the possibility of this sort of relationship had not before occurred to me. But then, some interesting notions popped into my head. If I thought about Sidney Bechet on the clarinet — all those sparkling treble trills, one display after another of pure expressional pyrotechnics — I found myself listening at the same time to specific *verbatim* passages from the novels of Stanley Elkin. And didn't the Canadian Brass sound a lot like Philip Roth? Superbly founded in musical fundamentals, determined to fully exploit the ranges of their instruments, they strut out onto the stage, stick their tongues into their cheeks, and proceed to address their audience as if musical performance were a competitive sport. The sound of Virgil Fox playing Bach — or maybe Haydn — on the Wanamaker Organ in Philadelphia put me in mind of the elegant, holy prose of Walker Percy. (Come to think of it, I've never heard Fox play Hovhaness on the Wanamaker, but if he did, I'll bet it would have sounded like Faulkner). And Vladimir Nabokov? He could have arranged the music on my beautiful Nicole Frères fat-cylinder overture music box. Pure voice, the singer become indistinguishable from his song.

I can't deny that I'd rather have recognized my own voice in the melodies of an elegant cylinder music box than in the windy, booming tones of a large band organ. A zesty serving of the driest cultivated epigrams, properly flavored with a delicate sprinkling of Attic salt, would have been greatly to my taste. But down in Roy Norman's basement, with that band organ blaring away at me, I realized that what I might have wished for simply was not going to happen. For some ten years, I'd been sitting at a typewriter, with my feet jammed as far as I could get them into a pair of lovely golden slippers, refusing to admit that the damned things were so painful that all I wanted was for the day's shift to end, so I could kick free of my constraints. I wondered whether I'd be able to even find my old clodhoppers any more, the ones that had once fit so comfortably. It had been such a long time since I'd stashed them away.

Roy was clearly disturbed at the way his creation had performed. His face was red; he was breathing heavily, and with a rasping noise. "Really needs the registers," he muttered. "They're all there, okay." He pointed at a little wooden box lying at the front of the organ, below the pipes. "Guess I shoulda hooked it up. But now, I'm not sure how . . ." His speech trailed off, and his eyes became distracted. "I don't have much music for it," he said. "I only made a few strips, just to work with. Y'know, you gotta punch out your own music for this organ to play."

My heartbeat went fast and irregular. I rubbed my chest and gulped air.

"Lemme see if I can get a longer strip," Roy said. "At least give you a better idea —"

"It's okay, Roy," I interrupted. "It's not necessary; I've heard enough. I want to buy the organ."

You could see the tension drain out of Roy's face and muscles. He smiled. "You do want it?"

I smiled back. "Yeah," I said. "Sure I want it."

"Well, that's great!" Roy pounded my shoulder as hard as he could. "Like I said, you're gonna have to punch out your own music, though. I got sixteen Wurlitzer rolls, they go with the deal, and you can transcribe them for this organ. I'll show you how."

He moved slowly across the basement toward the far back wall, and pointed definitively at a contraption that looked, I thought, rather like a crucified one-armed bandit. "This's the punch," he said. "Made it myself. You can transcribe any kind of roll onto a book for your organ over there."

It wasn't easy to follow Roy's presentation of his marvelous music-generating machine, because there was a concurrent monologue going on inside my head. "Roy," I finally said. "You say that your punch can transcribe music. I'll bet that a person could also use it to generate new arrangements of older music —couldn't he."

Roy looked puzzled. "I don't see why not," he said.

"And," I went on. "I'll bet he could even write new music altogether. *Compose* it, I mean."

Roy's expression indicated that he thought it was entirely possible — even likely — that he had entrusted his masterwork to a thorough nut case. What did I intend to do — sit there and punch out holes in a strip of cardboard, run the cardboard through the organ, screw my facial features into a knot, and then plug the holes I didn't like and replace them with new ones? And so on, till time immemorial? Maybe I *was* a young guy, Roy was probably thinking, at least by comparison to him. But wasn't I *looking* at him? Wasn't I listening? Sooner or later, time runs out. Who can afford to hang around and wait while a team of monkeys pounds away at typewriters, hoping for a chance association of letters that happens to read out as *Macbeth*?

But I wasn't thinking monkeys and typewriters. I was thinking MIDI. I was thinking music composition software. I was thinking a 63-note organ scale interposed between a computer and a synthesizer, filling a room with the kind of tweets, beeps, and grunts that could, once set up to near-satisfaction, be transferred to that cardboard. I was even thinking in terms of computer-directed cardboard punching. I knew, and very well, that unless I could somehow manage to link the machine-generated music of yesterday to that of today — or maybe even of tomorrow — I was sunk. Otherwise, there was no question that I'd be decomposing before I'd ever managed to compose. And I also knew that whether I really could transform my spur-of-the-moment theory into reality was problematic. No path between conception and creation is ever free of shadows, and the more twists and false turns there are in that path, the more grotesque will be the distortions of the light along the way.

But these shadows were my concern, and not something to trouble Roy with; he clearly had enough shadows of his own to think about right then. "Well, I guess I'd be smart to at least start with the transcribing, wouldn't I?" I said.

"Yeah," Roy grunted. "I'll show you how. When you come back for the organ."

While we were talking, Myra had come down the stairs. She was standing near the organ, looking closely at the eight giant trombone pipes. Talk about your moments of reckoning. "Pretty impressive piece of work, isn't it?" I said.

I had always wondered why the organ stop with a warbling, wavering, tremolo character is known as Vox Humana. All of a sudden, I knew.

"It's absolutely beautiful," said Myra. "And it sounds wonderful. Even from upstairs, the tone is so clear, so full." I realized she was looking at Roy, not at me. "You built this?" she said.

"Yup." Roy's speech was curt, even brusque, but his face was positively glowing. "Built it from scratch. There's wood in there, and pouch cloth, and leather; stuff you can't buy no more. But I found it, every bit of it. Wasn't gonna put nothin' in there that wasn't the best."

Myra nodded. "I can tell," she said quietly.

"We're going to buy it," I said, even more quietly. "Roy's agreed to sell it to us."

"I think that's great," said Myra.

Something was wrong, really wrong. This was not according to any known script. Such bizarre ad libbing should make a guilty collector very nervous indeed, and it did. But Roy interrupted my thoughts by telling us he wanted us to see the other organ. "Right in the next room, I'll show you." He shuffled off toward the doorway.

I followed him with less than moderate enthusiasm. I'd forgotten about that clock organ; why couldn't he have, too? And then, when we entered the room and I saw the thing, I felt even worse.

It looked like a clock organ, all right. Roy had it mounted on a small wooden platform, atop a home-made four-legged stand. It was weight-driven, as most of these machines are, and the brass works, all elegantly machined, were contained within a cage of brass plates to the right. Without question, it was an eighteenth-century machine, of the finest workmanship of that time. It might have been contained within a clock, set to play on the hour, but it also could have been hidden deep inside an *escritoire*, or writing desk. This was one of the loveliest dreams of the hard-core mechanical music collector. But the dream contained strong elements of nightmare. The thirty pipes, though perfectly crafted, were obviously new, as was the barrel. "Are the pipes the same as the original ones?" I asked Roy.

"They're better!" he said.

"I meant the tuning," I said quickly. "Is the scale the same?"

"I think so," Roy said. "Couldn't save the old ones; they were in too bad of a shape. "I made the new barrel; it's got *Music Box Dancer* on it."

I must have cringed, because Myra poked me — hard. But any sentiment, or appreciation for Roy's abilities aside, that remark was painful. Once upon a time, that organ might have played music by Mozart or Haydn; perhaps even an otherwise-unpreserved piece. Now, *Music Box Dancer*? The idea seemed actually perverse. I *couldn't* buy this one. Every time I'd look at it, I'd tear hair out of my scalp.

I was ready to tell Roy that I thought I'd settle for the big machine, but Myra interrupted me before I began. "You don't still have the original barrel, do you, Roy?" Myra asked.

I felt irritated, and stared at her. What a silly question. If he'd had the original barrel, why would he have made a new one?

"Sure I do," Roy said. "Over there in the corner. Couldn't ever get it to play right. So, I made a new one. Put *Music Box Dancer* on it, and it sounds pretty good."

Myra walked over to the far corner of the room, and brought back a little wooden barrel. All I could do was gawk. It clearly was the original source of music for this machine, and it appeared to be in very fine condition, the wood not split, and virtually all the metal pins and bridges in place and straight. What was going on here? Well, I knew that Roy was a builder, but he definitely was not a musician. In fact, I knew he'd always gotten help in setting up the scales for the organs he put together. He'd told me that he couldn't get the original barrel to "play right" —but he didn't have the original pipes or the original tuning scale. He would not have been inclined to go from barrel to pipes and back to barrel, working at retrieving and recreating the original scale. It just wasn't his thing. He knew how to make a better set of pipes, and probably a better barrel, too. And he liked *Music Box Dancer*. Well, okay; fair enough. But if a person were inclined, there were other collectors to talk to around the country and the world who'd have the proper range of expertise and experience to help in finding out just what sort of lost musical treasure might be on that wooden cylinder I was gripping with my white, shaking fingers.

"You can have that barrel, too, if you want it," said Roy.

We went upstairs, and I wrote Roy a check for the purchase of two mechanical organs.

In the car, on the way home, I made so bold as to tell Myra I was amazed at how readily she had accepted my new purchase. She shrugged. "Roy's daughters told me how he'd been working on it for all these years," she said. "And how badly he'd felt about not being able to finish it. And also how much he'd been hoping someone around here would take it on." She paused for a moment. "Besides, it really *is* a work of art; it's impressive as hell." She paused again, and then said, "And also besides, what would've been the point of saying no? If you'd gone home without either one of those machines, you'd be gnawing the legs off the furniture for weeks."

Not much I could say to that.

"What amazes *me*," my wife went on, "is that you were saying you thought you might try composing music for the organ? Did I hear you right? Why, you're fifty years old, and you've never in your life written a note of music."

"So what?" I said. "Joseph Conrad didn't know a word of English until he was a grown man — after he already spoke both Polish and French, by the way. But he *wrote* in English, didn't he? He said in his autobiography that it always felt natural to him to write in English — as if he'd been adopted in some mysterious way by the genius of the language."

"But still," Myra said. "You don't know the first thing about composing music."

Then, all of a sudden, she gave me that look. You know the look I mean: we get it all our lives. First from our mothers, and later from our wives. *What have you been up to?*

"Do you?" Myra asked, full of caution.

"Actually, yes," I said. "The first thing is that I want to. What I don't know is the second thing, and all the other things after that. But I think, maybe, I can just find them out. And if I do . . . well, just think about what a story *that* could make."

To her great and everlasting credit, Myra did not roll her eyes, sigh deeply, or snort. She confined her response to a smile, falling, I'd say, somewhere among amused, bemused, and mildly pained. After twenty-seven years of marriage, I suspect she's accepted that *cacoëthes scribendi* is an untreatable condition.

Just like collecting.

A hey-nonny-nonny and a hot-cha-cha
A vo-de-o-do and an oom-pah-pah.

Scribble, scribble!

The Story of a Hot Garbage Box,
or
Honesty May Be the Best Policy,
But It's Not Necessarily the Brightest

arbage boxes represent some of the later chapters in the story of the cylinder music box. They began to appear after about 1880, when the impressive artistic and technical accomplishments in the field were giving way to gimmickry and jim-crackery. Craftsmanship now yielded priority to production efficiency, as the third generation of music box manufacturers adopted what their descendants would a century later call a bottom-line orientation. Why use quality woods when cheap ones would really serve as well? Why spend all that time and money on fine marquetry and inlays when decals could be applied at considerably lower cost? Why set up intricate and beautiful music, when you could more easily divert the attention of the listener with cheap visual devices like drums, wood blocks, zithers, and enameled bell-strikers in the shape of birds or bees? And why construct sturdy tables with fine carving and other woodwork, when a rickety stand and a slathering of paint would do just as well? Increasingly, production managers came to hold sway over the tune arrangers, and, increasingly, the depressing voice of the garbage box was heard in the land.

Strictly speaking, there are two categories of garbage box. Both types are cylinder machines. The ordinary garbage box is one of those later, production-line machines which rendered (take that as you will) pedestrian arrangements of undistinguished music, and where no effort whatever was made to camouflage the discouraging mediocrity. The complex garbage box, on the other hand, is a more devious appurtenance — all full of untuned bells, drums, wood blocks, castanets, and other catchy visual gadgets to divert both the eye and ear of the listener, thereby drowning out the awful music. When H. L. Mencken wrote, some years later, that no one ever went broke by underestimating the public taste, he could have been holding aloft a garbage box as Exhibit A. *Res ipsa loquitur.* They sold by the hundreds of thousands.

Many people today, in fact, still prefer the garbage box to a high-quality, earlier musical cylinder. They will roll their eyes with boredom at the sound of a fine, 1860ish machine as it plays gorgeous arrangements of selections from Donizetti, Mozart, or Verdi; then they will proceed to rave about the wonderful music box they once saw, all full of shiny nickeled bells with pretty bee strikers, and neat drums, and a wood block with eight beaters that was a real hoot. And it played *good* music: you know, *Bicycle Built for Two, Home Sweet Home, Ta-ra-ra Boom-de-Ay,* and, oh yeah, *The Toreador Song. That's* the kind of music box *they'd* want if they were ever to buy one.

Well, *de gustibus non est disputandum.* One man's garbage may truly be another's treasure, and *vice versa.* Depends on the positioning of your viewpoint. But once judgement is made, the viewer should be consistent and true. Indulging in a little self-deceit is like being just a little bit pregnant: possible to keep under wraps, maybe, but only for a short time. Virtue is a demanding, uncomprising scold, and the person she most dearly loves to clout alongside the ear is the one who's willing to bend the rules of his own game. She's absolutely rigid, that one. Not an ounce of flexibility or a speck of compassion in her.

Listen to what she once did to me.

One evening last summer, I got a phone call from a man — let's call him Peter Sicuro — who identified himself as an insurance adjuster. He'd been referred by a mutual friend (who shall definitely remain nameless); this friend had told him that I knew something about music boxes, and could probably help him. Mr. Sicuro was representing a client who'd left a cylinder music box with an interior designer to have its warped lid repaired, but the box had been stolen from the shop. The client was more than a little upset, Sicuro said, since the music box was both magnificent and had been in the possession of the family for longer than a century. No one was holding out much hope for recovery, so the client wished to replace the box with one as similar as possible. Did I have something available?

I told Mr. Sicuro that it might help were he to describe the missing machine.

"Oh, it's a great big thing," he said. "Tremendous. Got one of those rolls in it, you know —"

"A cylinder?"

"Yeah. Whatever you call it. It's a good three feet long —"

"You *measured* that cylinder?" I asked. "And it's *three feet* long? Thirty-six inches?"

There was a brief pause. "Oh, it was a *good* three feet long. And it was inside of this incredible case — a real work of art. Gorgeous inlays all over it. They kept it sitting up on a big glass-top coffee table in the living room. And you should have heard the music that came out of it. Like nothing you've ever heard in your life. Played eight songs, I think."

A *glass*-top table? I thought. Not a stand, or a wooden table? "Was it an interchangeable box?" I asked.

"Huh?"

"Did it have more than one cylinder? You know, where you can take one out and put another one in, to play different songs?"

"Oh, I don't know," Mr. Sicuro said. "But it's got a jeweled movement."

I decided I'd heard enough. "Listen, Mr. Sicuro," I said. "I really don't think I can help you very much this way. I'd need to have a lot more, and clearer, information. But I can tell you that I definitely don't have anything here that would even be close to what you're describing. Maybe you'd like to bring your client over; he could look at what I do have for sale, and what's in my own collection. He could also look through some of my books and catalogs. If I had a better idea of what the box really looked like, I might be able to locate one."

"Yeah," Mr. Sicuro allowed. "Maybe I should do that. I can talk to him, and give you a call."

"And you might want to advertise in the music-box journals," I said. "Music boxes with three-foot-long cylinders are mighty scarce — which means it probably would actually be easier to recover it than to replace it. Because sooner or later, a box like that one is going to be offered to a collector."

"Nah, nah," said Mr. Sicuro. "It's gone. By now it's gotta be gone. They probably dumped it across the country, or maybe even in Europe, for all I know. Nah, at this point the best thing my client can do is just try to replace it. What kind of money do you think we'd be talking about?"

"I couldn't begin to tell you," I said. "You're an insurance adjuster — you wouldn't want me to give a careless answer like that, would you?"

"Oh, no, absolutely not. I don't want any answer at all, in fact. Just a ballpark estimate, absolutely unofficial. I'm curious."

"No way," I said. "If that box is really as big as you say it is —- *if* it's really that big — you could be talking as low as three thousand dollars, or as high as ten. *If* it's really the way you describe it. To give you any kind of a fair estimate, I'd need a hell of a lot more information than you've been able to give me."

"Fine," Mr. Sicuro said. "Thanks a lot. I'll be calling you."

The next weekend, while Myra and I were setting up our sales booth for Seattle's big semiannual antiques show, I noticed a young man giving our stuff more than a casual eye. He was small, and had dark hair, and he needed a shave. Finally, he began to speak. "Y' got a lotta music boxes, don't you?"

I resisted the urge to compliment him on his discerning eye, and simply replied, "That's what we sell."

"*We* had a music box stolen out of our shop last month," the young man said, and he mentioned the name of a local interior designer. "It belonged to one of our clients. He left it to get the lid straightened out; it was warped."

"Oh?" I said. I tried to not look terribly interested.

"One of our big customers,' the young man continued. He mentioned the name of one of Seattle's better-known, if not better-loved, citizens. "We got a contract to do over his whole house; we're talking hundreds of thousands of dollars. But now he's really sore, and he's cancelled some of the work. And he's trying to get us to pay for having the box replaced. His insurance agent is saying how it's worth at least three thousand dollars, but the guy himself says *he's* got an estimate for ten, and that's what he wants."

Oh, those sons of bitches! I thought. But all I said was a second "Oh?"

"Yeah. Ten thou! I'll tell you: I don't know anything about music boxes, really. But we've sold a couple, and they were nicer ones than that dog. And we didn't get anything like three thousand for them, and for sure, not ten. I'd love to know what it's *really* worth."

He was grinning at me now, and his eyes were glittering.

Once burned, twice cautious. "Can't help you," I said. "To have any idea at all, I'd have to see it and hear it." Then, I went back to setting out the display.

About a week and a half later, my phone rang at work. It was the owner of an antiques shop in my neighborhood; let's call him Sammy. "Larry!" he shouted into the phone. "Remember that music box I sold you a couple of months ago?"

Sure I remembered it. Sammy had called me at work then, too; he'd said he'd just gotten in a cylinder music box that I might be interested in. So, after work, I went over to see it. It was not exactly a machine to set a collector to drooling, though. In fact, it was a garbage box.

Sammy's machine fell into the ordinary-garbage-box category. The case had been painted over black, and the lid, with its ho-hum musical-instrument inlay, had been refinished with Varathane. You could have skated on it. The mechanism was a ten-tune, 17-inch cylinder, with a two-part comb; it played utterly-indifferent arrangements of ten la-de-da melodies. Six broken comb teeth had been replaced moderately well. As the box played, there were repetitive bird-like chirps and frog-like croaks, suggesting that the dampers were in need of replacement and/or adjustment. Nor could I recognize any of the tunes, since the tune card had apparently gone off with the entire Geneva mechanism to vanish into the black hole of the machine's history.

"I got it on commission from a little old lady," Sammy said. "Price is nine hundred, but you can have it for seven-fifty. That way, I'd be splitting my commission right down the middle with you."

I shrugged. "Oh, I don't know, Sammy," I said. "I don't like it. Frankly, it's just not a very good machine."

"Come on, come on, Larry." Sammy opened up his laryngeal grease spigot. "We been dealing for a long time; why're you trying to knock down my price? You know I do the best I can for you."

I knew nothing of the kind, but in this case it was a moot point. "No, really, Sammy," I said. "This is a just plain crummy box. You want me to tell you what's the matter with it?"

"Spare me." Sammy held up his hands, a cop at the conversational corner. "I know everything about music boxes I want to know, or need to know. And that's what they're worth. Now, look, Larry . . ."

"Yeah?"

"I also happen to know that you like to fix up music boxes, and that you don't exactly mind selling one here and there — isn't that right?"

I nodded.

"Okay, then. So, now, tell me this. After you're done fixing up this box so it's as good as it can be, what'll you be able to sell it for?"

This was a hard one. I have trouble once I'm past estimating the amount that a music machine is worth to me, and in that respect, this box wasn't worth much at all. Nor would it have been to any collector. But there are people, and a fair number of them, who want a music box — just a decent-playing garden-variety music box to put in the living room. It doesn't have to be anything special, because their interest is casual, and they don't want to spend an arm and a leg. "All right, Sammy," I said. "All fixed up, huh? For a one-box buyer, maybe $1500."

"Well, there you are, then." He punched my arm lightly. "You sure don't want to sell your real nice boxes, do you? Them, you want to keep yourself. So, are you gonna tell me that you wouldn't want to fix this box up right, and then turn around and sell it for double your money? In the first place, the repair work would be good practice for you. In the second place, there's seven and a half hundred bucks for you to spend on a box you'd want to keep. So, you're happy then, and the guy you sell the box to is happy — and so am I, and so is a little old lady who needs a little dough. Now, tell me: how can you not buy this box? Am I nuts, or are you?"

I studied the box for a moment. It did look like a proper challenge for my restoration skills, such as they were at that point.

Maybe Sammy was right. I said okay, and wrote a check. Then, I took the music box home.

During the next few months, I saw very little of Sammy. When he called me that second time at work, the agitation in his voice took me aback. "Yeah, sure I remember that music box," I told him. "I've got it fixed up, at least in as good shape as I can get it. I thought I'd take it to the Portland show in a couple of weeks and try to sell it."

There was a short pause, and then Sammy said, "Yeah, well, I guess Portland might be okay. But what I wanted to tell you is that you better not try to sell it in Seattle. That box is hot. It was stolen."

"*What* did you say?" I hadn't quite put it together; I thought I might have misunderstood Sammy. "Don't try to sell it around here, but *Portland* is all right? Is *that* what you're telling me?"

"Yeah . . . well, actually, Larry, if I was you, maybe I'd even hold it out of Portland right now. There was just a detective in here a few hours ago; they caught the guy who sold it to me. Turned out he lifted it from this interior decorator downtown — how do you like that, huh?"

All of a sudden, it came together, every bit of it, and I didn't like it in any way. Admittedly, people not familiar with music boxes do tend to see all cylinder machines as very similar. In spite of the fact that I have never run across two identical cylinder music boxes, most lay visitors to my collection appear to have had grandmothers who at one time owned music boxes *exactly* like the first one I show them. In addition, cylinder music boxes are at least the equal of fish when it comes to estimation of cylinder size. Subtract six inches from the declared length, and you may be close to the actual dimension. But still, my reason balked as I tried to figure out how an honest insurance agent could manage to turn that dreadful garbage box into a machine with a three-foot-long cylinder, playing the most wonderful music a person could imagine, and sporting a ten thousand dollar price tag. Especially now, in retrospect, when I recalled how thoroughly convinced said honest insurance agent was that the box was gone forever, and how uninterested he was in trying to recover it via an ad in a collectors' journal.

At that point, I wasn't sure which crook I was more eager to slug: Sammy or Mr. Sicuro "A *guy*, huh?" I shouted through the phone at Sammy. "You told me you had it on commission from a little old lady, remember? We split your commission. Isn't that right?"

Now, Sammy's voice got a little shaky. "No . . . no. I didn't say that. You didn't get it straight. See, the guy told me it was his grandmother's music box — that's where you must have got the little old lady bit from. But anyway, listen: how was I supposed to know the thing was stolen, huh? I bought it in good faith. I don't feel any personal responsibility. And, hey, listen: you'll be okay, too; don't worry. Just hold it out of Portland for now. Take it down there, say in the spring, and dump it then. Or, I know what — maybe you could just get rid of it real quietly through some of your music box collector pals. Call up some guy on the east coast, and sell it to him. Then, there won't be any problem at all, know what I mean? Everybody'll be okay."

I hung up the phone, looked up Mr. Sicuro's number in the Yellow Pages, and dialed it. When I told him I was in possession of his client's heirloom, I thought he might jump through the phone. "You bought it at Sammy's Antiques, huh?" he said.

I told him yes, and asked him how he knew.

"We caught the thief," Sicuro said. "He used to work at the interior designer's shop, until they found out he was taking little things here and there to buy himself drugs. So they set a trap for him, and he took the bait. He told the cops he sold the box to Sammy for two-hundred bucks." Sicuro chuckled. "It sounds like your friend Sammy wasn't too honest, either. He told the investigating detective he didn't know who it was that he sold the box to. He said he'd never seen the guy, and that he sold it for cash, and he didn't write a receipt. *Did* you pay cash?"

"No," I said. "I gave him a check. *And* I got a receipt."

"Good," said Sicuro. "We'll come by and pick up the music box from you. How much money have you got in it?"

"Seven-fifty," I said.

"Okay. Make a copy of your check and the receipt. We'll take care of you. The insurance company has authorized a reward for the return of the box. I'll see you tomorrow."

First thing the next morning, Mr. Sicuro appeared at the door; with him was a young woman who appeared to be suffering from St. Vitus Dance. Sicuro introduced her as Jenny Daniels, the proprietor of the interior design shop. I brought them both inside, and took them upstairs. As we entered a room containing perhaps twenty music boxes, Jenny let out a whoop and charged for the box Sammy had sold me. "That's it; that's *it!*" she screamed. For a moment, I was afraid that she might try to stuff the thing down the front of her blouse.

After the young woman had calmed down a bit, she explained that the owner had been pressing his claim with an unsettling degree of vehemence. Lawyers had even begun to materialize. "And we have no insurance," she said.

"No insurance?" I echoed. "How can you not have insurance."

She shot me a dose of irritated condescension. "Do you have any idea how expensive insurance would be?" she said.

"No," I said. "Only how expensive it might not be."

She glanced at the music box. "How much do you think that music box *might* be worth?" she said.

Her name went immediately onto my Wishful Hit List. "Well," I said, "To somebody who doesn't want a music box, nothing. To someone who can't live without it, maybe a million. Otherwise, someplace in between." I looked at Mr. Sicuro, and added, "The cylinder's not *quite* three feet long."

He smiled, a little lamely, and then shrugged. "I only saw it once; that's how big it looked to me."

My visitors signed a receipt for the music box, and then they departed, music box clutched firmly in Jenny Daniels's fists. Mr. Sicuro waved the copies of the check and receipt back at me. "I'll be in touch," he said. "Don't worry. We'll take good care of you."

Two days later, I received a curt note from Mr. Sicuro, thanking me for being such a nice, honest fellow, and suggesting that I might do well to talk to Sammy about getting my money back. A quick phone call to Mr. Sicuro brought a vague explanation that the insurance company was not being terribly cooperative, and that there were "problems."

"I thought the insurance company had authorized a reward," I said. "Is there a problem with that, now, too?"

"You know what?" Mr. Sicuro said. "You think you're a real wise guy, don't you? Well, I don't like your attitude, and I'm not inclined to listen to any more of this." And with that, he hung up the phone.

A few days later, Jenny Daniels called to tell me how relieved she was to get the music box back to the owner, and thereby to get the owner off her back. "Don't forget," she said. "If there's anything I can do to help you get back your money, I want you to let me know right away."

"Well, I said. "Since it sounds as if you were looking at a loss of three, or maybe ten, thousand dollars until I came along, perhaps *you* might write *me* a check for $750. And then *you* could try to recover from Sammy. What do you say?"

"Oh, no! I couldn't do *that.*" She sounded positively horrified. "You're the one who bought the music box from him, so you're the only one who has recourse there. But I'll do whatever I can to help you — all you have to do is call me."

In most stage presentations, the cops are listed pretty close to the end of the *dramatis personae*, since they usually appear at that point where the reasonably thickened plot needs a bit of a fresh stir. In this respect, my particular theatre of the absurd proved no exception. While my pendulum of temper was swinging fiercely between trying to figure out the move which would bring down the most birds with the least shot, and just quietly chalking up the whole damned episode to experience, I received a phone call from Detective Charles Simon, of the Fraud Unit. To say that the detective was upset would be roughly akin to remarking that Napoleon was ambitious. "I don't like being lied to," Simon said. "So, I'm telling you, I want to nail your pal Sammy good. Now, *you* tell *me* exactly what were the circumstances of your buying that music box from him."

I went through the entire transaction, pausing every so often to let the detective splutter. When I finished, he said, "Okay . . . okay. Now, you're sure that's *exactly* how it went?"

"I won't vouch for direct quotes," I said. "But outside of that, yes."

"*Okay*, then!" he repeated. "Now, listen. Sammy told me this guy brought the music box in, and said he was selling it for his grandmother. So, Sammy paid him two hundred bucks. Then, he said that he sold it for cash to a customer he'd never seen before, and has never seen afterward, and he didn't give a receipt. So, right there, there's a lie. And then you say he called you right up, told you the box was stolen, and advised you to dump it off onto the East Coast. Now, here's what I'm going to do. I'll have your statement typed up; then, I'll want you to read it over and sign it. And then, I'm going to go visit Sammy again, and ask him to repeat what he told me, for the record. That way, I'll catch him in his lie –- and even more. You need to get your money back from Sammy, right? Well, I'm going to tell him that I have enough evidence to file obstruction of justice charges against him, and that if he has any sense at all, he'll return you your money, and fast. It'd look a lot better for him in court, and he'd be awfully stupid if he doesn't see that."

I mentioned that I was not particularly thrilled at the notion of what Sammy might decide to pull off by way of revenge.

"Oh, no problem," the detective said genially. "I'll tell him that he is to have no contact with you whatsoever — and I don't want *you* to talk to *him* at all, either. I'll also let him know straight out that if, say, your house ever gets trashed, why he's going to be the first suspect."

I thought that somehow, that sounded less than completely comforting.

"In a way, it's too bad," Detective Simon went on. "It sounds as if you're the only person in this whole mess who did the right thing, and you're also the only one who's out of pocket. You do know, don't you, that since you didn't buy that box directly from the thief, you actually had a legal claim on it? If you hadn't been so nice and just returned it, the owner would have had to take *you* to court, and it would have been a real hassle to get the whole thing sorted out. Didn't the owner even offer to pay you what you're out?"

"I've never talked to the owner," I said.

"He didn't even call to say thank you?" Simon sounded incredulous.

"Uh-uh."

"Christ," said the detective. "What a world this is. Well, look: I'll do what I can to help you."

"Everyone's falling over everyone else to help you get the money from somebody else," Myra said sourly.

"Well, at least this guy is the first one who can't say somebody else, not me," I said. I thought Myra seemed less than impressed. Not that I could blame her.

A couple of weeks passed; then, a couple more. I called Detective Simon. Oh, yes, sure he remembered me. But he'd had to change his plan. "I thought about it later," he said. "And I don't want Sammy to know in advance that I know he's lying. I don't want him to have any chance to cover over his tracks before all this gets to court. So, why don't you do it this way: go talk to him now. Just plain tell him you want your money back. Maybe he'll be running scared enough to give it to you. But if he's not, well then, go and file in Small Claims Court. You'll certainly collect there. Why, you couldn't possibly lose."

I know I rolled my eyes. Once again, I wondered whether I'd be smart to just chuck the whole business, and get on with other things.

"Do you want to let that son of a bitch Sammy pick your pocket, and just walk away scot-free?" demanded my mild-mannered spouse. "*I'd* like to kill him, the dirty dog."

I allowed that she had a valid point. "No, I really don't," I said. "But if you want to know the truth, I'm less mad at Sammy than I am at everybody else here. Sammy's just a two-bit crook; he's made that more than obvious, and I'll take him for what he is. But all those other people? I get Jenny Daniels off a ten-thousand dollar hook, and she tells me she's just awful sorry that I'm stuck for seven-fifty, but it ain't *her* problem. And that bum Sicuro and his pal, the owner? They're probably pissing and moaning all over Seattle about that idiot music box collector who had to go and return their lousy garbage box and cost them ten K, plus maybe another five for lost sentimental value. *Those*'re the people I'd really love to stick it to. But Sammy's the only one I have any kind of a legal claim against. So, no. I guess I *could* chuck it — but I don't think I could forget about it. I'll go have a talk with Sammy."

Though his shop is hardly in a bad neighborhood, Sammy keeps the door locked; when I rang the bell, he hustled me inside as though he were afraid I might let in the plague. "*Lar*-ree; hey, how y' doin'?" he chirped. Then, he made a show of looking me over. "He-e-y, now — I bet I know what you're here for, right? You're gettin' worried about that hot music box, and you want to return it. Well, no trouble, no trouble at all. Just bring it on in, and I'll give you back your money. I'll take care of it. It doesn't make *me* nervous at all."

"Well," I said. "You're partly right. "I do want my money back. But I can't give you back the box."

Sammy looked at me like a curious sparrow on a telephone wire. "Why not?"

"Because I returned it," I said.

"You what?" His jaw hung loosely, and his eyes were utterly uncomprehending.

"I returned it, Sammy," I said. "You know –- I gave it back to the owner."

Sammy started to wave his arms; I thought he might be warming up to toss a full-scale tantrum. "You . . . you . . ." he began, and then, collecting himself, he shouted, "What the hell did you do a thing like *that* for?"

"What did I *do* it for?" I had to stop for a moment. Sammy's bewilderment was so complete, and so genuine — perhaps the most honest reaction I'd ever gotten from him — that it threw me off my stride. Clearly, this man believed that I had been born yesterday, and with a serious congenital malformation of my brain as well. What *did* I do it for? "Well, I guess because I'd hope that if some other collector had been sold one of *my* music boxes, he'd do the same thing for me," I said. "I just don't like to think that a music box collector could ever enjoy a machine he knew had been stolen."

That seemed to wrap up the situation for Sammy. Initial diagnosis confirmed: retarded infant at large. Back to business. His eyes narrowed, and his face tightened. "*When* did you return that thing?" he said.

"Right after you called me," I snapped. "About a month and a half ago."

Back to confusion. The only clear message on Sammy's face represented the notion that if he had to do business with morons like this, it just wasn't worth the aggravation. "Well, then, what the hell are you coming here *now* for?" he said.

"Because the cop who talked to you also came and talked to

me," I said. "And he told me not to have any kind of contact with you — that is, until yesterday. Then, he said it'd be okay to talk to you about getting my money back."

As I watched Sammy's face, it occurred to me that he might have gone into a life of petty crime to pay off debts from the poker table. Because he certainly was no card sharp. "Whattaya *mean*, the cop said you shouldn't have any contact with me?" Sammy barked. "Why not?"

I shrugged. Even mentally defective newborns are not utterly devoid of protective reflexes. "How do *I* know?" I said. He told me he was investigating the case. Whatever that meant."

Sammy's voice went from bark to growl. "What the hell did you *tell* that cop, huh, Larry?"

"I told him what happened," I said. "Listen, what do you think? *I'm* not dumb enough to lie to a cop who's investigating a robbery."

"Oh . . . so *you're* not dumb enough, huh?" From menacing growl to the patronizing sneer of superiority. "*I* go and put myself at risk to protect *you*, and then, as far as you're concerned, that's just dumb. That's the thanks I get. Real nice, Larry!"

Unfortunately at that point, I started to laugh. Whether this righteous indignation on Sammy's part was sincere — an expression of dismay at the breakdown of honor that should exist among thieves — or whether it was simply another dissimulation, I couldn't tell. In either case, it struck me as very funny. "Come on, would you, Sammy," I said. "*You* were trying to protect *me*? From what? *I* didn't buy a stolen music box, and then fence it. I bought it in good faith from a supposedly reputable antiques dealer, who ought to have every legal and moral obligation to give me back my money as soon as he finds out that the merchandise was stolen."

"Well, that's what I told you to do," Sammy said. "When I called you up, I told you to bring it back, and I'd give you back your money. So, where have you been, huh?"

Good move, Sammy. Now, the confusion was all mine. "That's bullshit, and you know it," I shouted. "What you told me was that you had no problem, and you felt no obligation. You told me I should dump the box on the East Coast. Get it out of this area. Then, we'd both be just fine."

Sammy rolled his eyes, and waved his hand in a flowery dismissal. "Oh, come on, Larry. I *never* told you to do that. I told you to just bring the box back, but you didn't want to. You were smelling money then, and you figured you'd make a quick little profit and be clean out of the deal. But then you got scared, didn't you? So you returned the box to the owner, and decided that maybe if you acted like Mr. Goody-Goody, you could at least break even and leave *me* holding the bag. Well, shit! I'm not about to hand you over a check, so you can just go and turn *that* over to the cops, too. Why, if I give you back your money now, then that incriminates *me*; it's like I'm just out and saying I'm guilty. Go on. Get your chickenshit ass the hell out of here. Quit being such a cry-baby. Take your medicine. It ain't *my* fault you tried to screw around, and then lost your nerve. Beat it. Don't come back, either. Business like yours I can do without."

"Okay," I said. "I'll see you in Small Claims Court, then. We can go in front of a judge, and then we'll see who's going to feel incriminated."

"Good," Sammy said. "I'll see you in court — that is, if you think you've got the balls for it. I just don't want to see you in here no more, okay? The stink keeps out the *good* customers."

Once again, I wondered whether I *should* just take my medicine. A person really ought to expect to pay for his education. Oh, those lousy garbage boxes! Maybe I *will* drop it, I thought. Forget Small Claims Court. By the time I'm done, even if I win in money, I'm going to lose, and bigger, in time and aggravation.

"Is that what you're going to do, then?" Myra asked.

"Uh-uh," I said. "No. Common sense tells me yes, but I just can't. Not now. Not after everybody in this whole case has taken such a nice, big turn at my screw. And not after Sammy talked to me like that."

"What did you think?" Myra said. "That you were going to walk back into that shop, and a slimebag like Sammy was going to tell you how sorry he was, hand over a check for the full purchase price, and swear eternal mending of his sinful ways? Maybe you really *were* born yesterday."

"I thought," I said, a little more emphatically than I'd have liked, because I was feeling more than a little foolish. "I thought he might be smart enough to figure that legally, he was stuck, and that besides, if this thing ever *does* come to court — *any* court — he'd look a hell of lot better if he had voluntarily returned my money."

Myra snorted. "A creep like that never figures he's stuck, legally or any other way," she said. "Only people like you and me get stuck legally. Guys like that win cases they should lose, because they *are* such good liars. And even when they do lose, they refuse to pay, and then go and try to get the money out of them. What's your leverage? Debtor's prison? Push them too hard, and they just vanish. Next week, Sammy could be selling hot music boxes in L. A. Or Brazil. What would he care? The world's his oyster. And what he likes to do most of all is spit it right in other peoples' eyes."

"He's spit enough in mine already," I said. "My turn." Then, I went downtown to Small Claims Court, and filed my case.

A few weeks later, the mailman delivered a thick manila envelope from an attorney's office. The attorney in question was Sammy's, and she was notifying me of her motion to transfer the case to a District Court. Why? Because Sammy's intention was to countersue me for slander and libel, in relation to the remarks I had allegedly made to a police officer.

So, at that point, of course, I called *my* lawyer. My description of the situation seemed to both amaze and amuse him. "The guy doesn't have a leg to stand on," he said. "After all, you *did* return the music box right after he called you –- that's on the record. And it's pretty clear that he *did* lie to a police officer, and that's about the worst thing a person could have going against him in a court hearing. And also, there's no way a person can be sued successfully for *any* remarks he makes to a policeman during his investigation. If he could, no one would ever talk to a cop. A judge certainly would consider that to be an immune, or privileged, communication. So, I'm sure you'd win. What this character obviously thinks is that he can scare you off with the countersuit. But what are we talking about here –- you said $750, right?"

"Yes," I said. "And you're probably going to tell me to forget it; it's not worth the time and the aggravation. But I'm going to tell you that at this point, I'm going to be more aggravated if I *don't* follow through. So, let's go ahead. If he wants District Court, let's give him District Court."

My lawyer sighed. "That's what they all say," he said. "Well, you do know, too, don't you, that the only one who's going to make any money out of this is me."

"I've thought of that," I said. "And let's put it this way. I'd rather see the dough in your pocket than in Sammy's. Lesser of two evils. All right?

He laughed. "Have it your way. But actually, maybe you just *might* get something out of it. If this Sammy character really does want to go ahead, I don't see how he can avoid perjuring himself -- there are so many inconsistencies and outright lies in his story. He could end up with criminal charges being brought against him. He could even go to jail."

"Great," I said. "Be worth it at twice the price. I think he'd look terrific in stripes."

Now, it was between Sammy's lawyer and mine. The opposition more than intimated that in court, they would sufficiently embarrass the respected physician such that he'd have trouble earning his living, once whatever it was they had to tell about him was splashed all over the front pages of the local newspapers and on TV screens. I said let them try. Then, they told my lawyer that it was hypocritical of me to behave as if I were a Boy Scout, and why didn't I just accept the ways of the world? Sammy, being the fine fellow he was, would show his good faith by refunding me half the cost of the music box. We'd share the loss, like two understanding businessmen should. I said I'd see Sammy in hell first, let alone in court. Finally, the afternoon before the scheduled hearing, my lawyer called me. "They've agree to settle," he said. "They'll withdraw their claim, and pay the cost of the music box. I guess they're not quite as dumb as I thought."

"I guess I should be glad," I said. "But you know what: I'm disappointed. I was really looking forward to getting them into court, and watching Sammy wiggle around in that witness chair while you were giving him the business."

The lawyer laughed. "Actually, I'm a little disappointed myself," he said. "Lawyers aren't supposed to take this stuff personally, but my opponent has been so ridiculous about the whole thing that I was kind of looking forward to court myself. But figure it this way, though. Without having to go to court, you'll end up with about half of the settlement, instead of me getting the whole thing. So, take the money, why don't you. You might as well. You're sure not going to get any more satisfaction out of this mess."

He was right. The fact that Sammy's loss on the garbage box was twice mine (even more, if you figure in *his* legal fees) wasn't the least bit satisfying. Even Virtue welched on me: in the end, she delivered no more reward than did Mr. Sicuro's insurance company. I felt like a schmuck, not a saint.

Sammy would take a nice tax write-off for his business loss. The thief would get a few weeks of free bed, breakfast, and Methadone at the County Facility, and would then be released on probation to his social worker. Conniving Mr. Sicuro would probably receive the Agent of the Month Award from his appreciative company. Mealy-mouthed Jenny Daniels likely would sweet-talk her client into continuing the hundred-thousand-dollar restoration project, and forgetting about the 10K lawsuit. And that client, the ungrateful son of a bitch! *He* had his family heirloom back, free and clear. Once again, the treasure of his forefathers rested in its proper place of honor, on the glass-topped coffee table in the living room. The garbage box, home to roost.

But that, of course, was the whole point, and who but myself did I have to blame? Having judged it a garbage box, I bought it anyway, so that any reasons I might have thought I'd had for the purchase were in fact only excuses. What kind of treasure did I really expect to find in a garbage box? When a person lowers his face to take swill out of a trough, he'd better be ready to fight off the pigs. And in the end to leave his shirt at the cleaners.

So, I decided to put aside that remark from Detective Simon, the one about the only person who did the right thing being the one who came out on the short end. The person who came out on the short end was the only one who knowingly, and in cold blood, acted in a manner inconsistent with his own beliefs and values. No wonder there were no rewards forthcoming, even from Virtue. *Especially* from Virtue. I figured that rather than feeling cynical and morally superior, I'd do better to be grateful for having gotten off as easily as I did.

The God in the Music Box

Reason and Mysticism, those polar stars of the mind, have been at war forever, and likely forever will be. What's more, this struggle is total. Between Logic and Belief, there is no middle ground, no field for possible compromise. A single belief, immediately upon acceptance, will weaken a logical structure to the point of collapse. And on the other hand, a belief explained is a belief destroyed.

True belief has nothing to do with evidence, whether corroborative or contradictory. We don't, after all arrive at our beliefs; we simply—and suddenly—believe. Just like that. From one instant to the next, without choice, without decisions. Doubt for an instant, and Belief turns her back upon you. Say maybe, and you find yourself barreling along, helter-skelter, through a dark chute, and when you emerge once again into the light, you find yourself staring directly into the unblinking eyes of Logic.

So, we're either in one camp or the other, never both at once. But occasionally, we do find ourselves standing on a queer bit of unmarked turf, a small patch of *terra incognita* of the mind. Under these unsettling conditions, it is no small task to regain our bearings and figure out which army is in fact the legitimate occupying force of that particular territory. Believe me; I know. I've been there. Let me tell you what happened to me, a few years back, when I found myself entangled in an odd situation involving two brothers at odds, a wonderful music box, and the Cosmic Forces.

Once, there were two young men in Denver who were brought together by their interest in music boxes. One was Elton Norwood, a gifted musician and puppeteer; the other was David Wells, a talented sculptor. As the acquaintance ripened into friendship, the men discovered that they also shared a prodigious aptitude for music-box repair work; in fact, they realized very early on that the emotions they experienced while restoring fine cylinder boxes were of a distinctly spiritual quality. To set up shop together, then, seemed the most reasonable thing in the world. The young men gave their collaborative venture the name Freres de Metatron, an apt choice, in that the archangel Metatron, the designated Master of Heavenly Song, is also supposed to stand as the link between the human and the divine.

It was a felicitous association. Working together, Elton and David developed their skills with astonishing speed and facility, such that by the early nineteen-eighties, music box collectors generally acknowledged that they had no peers. Superb cylinder boxes in disrepair which had been closely guarded for years against the day that the restorer of restorers would appear began to come out of closets all over the country. Shipped to Denver in baskets, they returned to their owners in glory.

Not that the work was easy—it wasn't. Sometimes the brothers became so engrossed in a particular project that they forewent meals, and worked straight through the day. At times, they chose to work through the night as well. But then, there was always that moment when they released the stop detent from a cylinder, and for the first time listened to that particular comb sing. Then, exhaustion gave way to exhilaration. They surprised their patrons by their inability to recall whether it had been Elton or David who had originally conceived a specific ingenious little technique, or whether it was David or Elton who'd first made a certain critical observation. Their capabilities and their potential seemed limitless.

But whom the gods would destroy, they first label promising. Brilliantly talented though the brothers were, they were still two people, with two minds and two mindsets. The approach of each brother to the restoration work developed and matured along increasingly divergent paths, and as time went by, they found themselves increasingly unable to resolve their philosophical differences. By the autumn of 1988, David had left the workshop; in fact, he was no longer even a member of the Musical Box Society. Meanwhile, Elton's solitary star had gone on for a time to burn more brightly than ever, But now he lay wasted and helpless, dying slowly of an incurable disease.

As one who joined the Musical Box Society in 1986, I was amply familiar with and respectful of Elton Norwood's restoration work. But he and I were no more than the most casual of acquaintances, and so, my feelings with regard to his terminal illness went no further than ordinary human sympathy and regret. Thus, one evening, in late October, when my friend Maury Willyard called and told me that Elton had died the previous evening, I felt only that emotion a person might have, say, on the passing of a writer whose work he particularly enjoyed and respected. Maury went on to say that he'd heard the news from Olin Tillotson, a mutual friend and a scholar of cylinder music boxes, who lives in Vancouver, Canada. "Olin also asked me to tell you that there's a Malignon available," Maury went on to say. "He thought you might be interested."

Now, I felt emotion. I nearly dropped the phone.

"Olin has heard the box, and seen it," Maury said. "He told me it's out of this world—one of the best around. It's for sale because the owner needs to raise some money. Do you want the name and number to call?"

"Definitely," I said.

Maury read a phone number to me. "The name of the owner is David Wells," he said.

I thanked Maury, and hung up; then, I picked the receiver back up and began to hit buttons frantically. My finger touched the six instead of the nine. I muttered an unpleasant word, slammed down the receiver, and grabbed it right up again.

"What *is* the matter?" Myra said. She had come into the room, and was eyeing me in a curious manner. "Who are you calling in such a hurry?"

"There's a Malignon for sale," I shouted, as I started to assault the buttons once again.

"Oh, God!" Myra went pale, and scurried into the living room to sit down, safely out of my way.

Now, what ever might a Malignon be, you may ask, that a wife would sooner jump in front of a steamroller than place herself in the path of a collector—even her husband—as he moved to pursue the thing. Alphonse Malignon was a Swiss watchmaker who lived from 1800 to 1875; he may also have made at least a few music boxes, since his name is known to appear on approximately twenty examples throughout the world. Each of these boxes is a keywind, and each is characterized by outstanding details of workmanship. As regards both the quality of the musical arrangements and the tone of the music, every Malignon cylinder is right up there at the front of the very first rank. There are those in music box circles who would have the rest of us believe that Malignon was an imposter of sorts—that he was no more than the distributor of the boxes which bear his name. This mechanical music version of the Shakespeare/Bacon controversy holds that the fine music boxes marked with the names Metert, Moulinie, and Malignon were, in reality, manufactured by another Swiss firm, that of Langdorff. Yet, there are those of us who place more stock in the immutable and unfakable individuality of voice. One evening, as I was reviewing a tape containing the music of several Malignon boxes, Myra, who'd been reading in the room, suddenly looked up from her newspaper and said, "*That* one doesn't sound like a Malignon."

It wasn't, I told her. It was a Metert, gratuitously thrown in by my correspondent.

Thus rests the defense! *Res ipsa loquitur.*

But whatever the truth, the fact remains that Malignon boxes are neither large nor showy; thus, unless you were a certified cylinder fanatic, you probably would not go far out of your way to own one. But if you were such a lunatic, you'd go barefoot to the end of the earth.

David Wells' telephone voice was deep, rich, and vibrant. Yes, he did have a Malignon box for sale, and of course he was pleased that a friend of Olin Tillotson's might be interested in it. He said that he thought it was unusually nice, in that it had both a forte-piano comb setup, and a nest of 13 hidden bells. Real cylinder collectors *hate* bells. These collectors can be counted upon to gag audibly when exposed to a large music box with a nest of six, nine, or twelve bells, sometimes struck by beaters in the shape of birds, bees, or Oriental mandarins holding gong-sticks. These bells are usually quite loud, and tend to drown out the music from the comb—which the real cylinder collector might claim to be an act of charity, in that the musical arrangements in these boxes tend to be highly undistinguished. However, the first bells to be placed in music boxes (c. 1850) were hidden down beneath the bedplate, out of sight, and they were tuned and their notes set up so as to make the bell music an integral part of the arrangement. I didn't need to be told that the bells in a Malignon music box would be both hidden and excellent.

David told me that he'd owned the box for about ten years; he'd acquired it in very poor condition, and had restored it in 1980. "I'd been doing full restoration jobs for about a year then," he said. "I had to repin the cylinder, replace a tooth on the comb, and reset the combs—and, oh yes. I had to tune the bells and set them up. And then, of course, the usual dampering; I thought it would take forever. And the case. I completely redid the case."

This little speech set me far back on my heels. Only the fact that Olin Tillotson knew both the Malignon and its owner kept me from hanging up the phone. Was I really supposed to believe that one of this person's first complete restoration projects involved a Malignon, and that it had turned out superbly? He might as well have told me that he'd happened to wander into the British Museum one morning, taken a look at the damaged Portland Vase, rolled up his sleeves, gone to work, and finished a perfect restoration job in time for dinner. "Well, fine," I said. "But let me ask a question. Who *are* you, anyway?"

I heard a nervous laugh at the other end of the line.

"I'm sorry," I said quickly. "It's just that...well, I've never heard of you. I know a fair number of music box people, and I figured I'd have at least heard of a person who's good enough to do a Malignon as one of his first repair jobs. But I've never heard of *you*."

"Well, but I *do* restore music boxes," David said. "I was associated with another restorer here in Denver. Maybe you've heard of *him*. His name was Elton Norwood. He...died. Last night."

So, that was the link between the two messages from Olin. I had that terrible feeling a person gets when he opens the door to a bathroom or a bedroom at just the wrong moment. I stammered something about not knowing, and maybe we should talk some other time.

"Oh, no," said David. "Not at all. "It isn't as though it were a terrible shock—unfortunately, I've known for a long time that it was going to happen. And as sick as Elton was...well, you know. In a way, it's kind of a relief."

In my business, you know, all right, and too well. "Yes," I said. "I understand."

"And besides," David continued. "I'm enjoying talking to you. Let's just go on, why don't we."

So, David went on to tell me about the Malignon. He reiterated that it was a forte-piano box, and that there was a large nest of bells, hidden away under the bedplate. "In fact," David said, "in the first tune, the *Stradella* Polka, by Strauss, the music begins with a bells solo. It's beautiful. Like a carillon, actually. I think this is the only bells solo I've ever heard on a music box."

David explained that he'd bought the box for the express purpose of restoring it. That done, he had never intended to sell. "But it's a necessity," he said. "Frankly, it's the only thing I have that will bring me the money I need right now."

My acquisitional enthusiasm flagged, if only a bit. Sometimes, it's difficult for a collector to accept that people don't sell their top-quality items just for the hell of it. Once David had restored that music box, he'd vested an interest in it in a nontransferrable currency, and for him to need to sell it came across simply as wrong. In a terribly important sense, the box was his and his only.

Nevertheless, very few of us are so constituted that we will send a large sum of money to a total stranger, with the stipulation that he keep his special music box. And David had to know that this was not a reasonable hope. Clearly, he had struggled hard, and he'd finally come to the decision that he must sell, so sell he would.

It might as well be to me.

I asked him his price.

Now, David began to stammer. It really was next to impossible, he said, to arrive at a fair price for such a music box, there being so fe specimens by this particularly fine maker known to exist. Of course, he wanted to get as much as he could, but he did want to be fair, and so he'd asked the advice of knowledgeable friends throughout the country.

Finally, he named the number. I felt staggered. It was more than I'd ever paid for a music box—but then again, so what? Had I ever bought a Malignon? David was right: how *does* a person really go about setting a fair and reasonable price for an object at once so rare and so wonderful?

"Are you…still there?" David said.

"Yes…yes," I replied. "I'm here. Just reacting."

David let out a very nervous laugh. "Well, I know it *is* a lot of money," he said. "Would you like me to send you a tape, perhaps? I can record the box tomorrow, and I have some pictures, too. Also, I'll send you a photocopy of the article I wrote about the box for the M.B.S.I. Journal, back in 1980. I suspect I can get it all in the mail by tomorrow afternoon, and then, you can look it over and listen…

I was concentrating on what David was saying, trying to make some sort of reasonable assessment of the situation, but right at that point, I interrupted him by blurting out, "Mr. Wells, I'll buy your music box."

I *say* I said it, but I hadn't realized I actually *had* said it until I heard the words being spoken. It felt as if someone else were speaking through my vocal cords. A psychiatrist would claim that this represented some form of dissociation on my part, a splitting off of myself from the agent who would have to make and take responsibility for the decision. And maybe the psychiatrist would be right.

Now, it was David who was silent. "Are *you* there?" I said.

"Well, yes," he said. "Yes...yes. But, uh...really! Don't you want me to send you the pictures and a tape? You don't want to buy it just like that, do you? I'll tell you what: *let* me send—"

I interrupted him again. "No, I've made up my mind," I said. "I'm going to buy your box—that is, if you do want to sell it to me. I know Olin well enough to go on his assessment, so I'll send you a check tonight. Let's say it's settled."

We talked a while longer. David said he'd send me the pictures and the tape anyway, but insisted that he would not ship the music box. "I want to fly out to Seattle, and deliver it personally," he said. "I want to put it directly into your hands." So, we arranged that he would come and spend the weekend after next with us.

At one-thirty that morning, I slipped quietly out of bed, so as to not wake Myra, and padded up to the living room. Insomnia is a frequent caller on me; we are well acquainted, and so I felt I was showing no disrespect by stretching informally across the sofa. I looked around the room, taking in the dark shapes of my silent music boxes. My mind was in a ferment; thoughts bubbled, pell-mell, to the surface. What was I doing? Was I crazy? Didn't I have enough music boxes? And my God: all that money! Without seeing; without hearing. What if I didn't like the box—should I go tell Olin Tillotson to lend me his ears?

But a Malignon. Music boxes don't get better than Malignons. And if that's the case, then what *is* a Malignon worth—at least to a collector of cylinder music boxes? There are people who've been collecting for thirty years who don't have a Malignon, and who would kill for one. In a situation like this, you *can't* hesitate; turn around to think, and your chance is gone—maybe forever. *Carpe diem.*

Hoo-hah. *Carpe diem*! he says. Seize the day, huh? Well, if you're in the mood to sling platitudes, why don't you try fools rush in.

But I *didn't* rush. I'll admit, I moved pretty promptly, but I didn't rush. From what David Wells told me over the phone, I not only can see that box, I swear I can *hear* it. The whole program. With the forte-piano combs, and the bells, I can hear it. I've heard other Malignons, and I can hear what this one will sound like. So, I *didn't* rush. Not at all. We talked about it for more than an hour.

On your nickel. But never mind. Would this be the first time you've been screwed by someone who came highly recommended? Seeing—and hearing—really *are* believing; making assumptions is foolish and dangerous. And also—there *is* such a thing as a bad Rolls Royce, or a bad Mercedes, isn't there? You can't talk cars. There are more than seventeen Mercedes and Rollses out there. And even luxury cars come off production lines. If you want to make comparisons, ask whether there are bad Rembrandts, or bad Van Goghs.

Well, of course there are; you *know* there are. But collectors who have more money than brains buy them anyway, and hang them up on their walls, and then adore them because they *are* Van Goghs, or they *are* Rembrandts. Look, for all that money, why the hell didn't you just catch a plane and fly out to Denver to hear the thing before you said yes? The price of a plane fare sounds like pretty cheap insurance to me.

I pay too damn many insurance premiums already. My house, my cars, my belongings, my ability to work, my life— they're all insured to the gills. Isn't there *anything* a person can do without insurance? For a basic trapeze routine two feet off the ground, you just plain don't need a safety net. In fact, you'd look ridiculous.

But what was the hurry? What was the *hurry*?

The thermostat was turned down for the night, and the sweat running down my back turned almost immediately icy. I was starting to shiver. This had all the promise of a night-long stand, six hours in the living room with Insomnia, until, at the dawn's early light, my guest would excuse himself and leave me to shave, eat breakfast, and drag off for a zombie's day at the office. But just at that point, I heard a voice—- or, more properly, I *discerned* a voice. The sensation was somewhere between genuine hearing and imagination, the sound seeming to originate from within my own head. But not from my mind; it felt as though it had been processed by the usual auditory pathways. With the exception of directionality, all the characteristics of a spoken voice were there. The closest I can come to an accurate description would be to say it was as if I'd suddenly plunked a set of earphones into place, while a compact disc player at the other end of the wire was in operation.

The voice said: "This is what I intended."

Just that. No more. And although the voice itself was not a particularly soothing one—in fact, it was imperious almost to the point of harshness—the message came across as immensely calming. My second odd vocal experience within a few hours! This time, that consulting psychiatrist would probably venture the opinion that I had copped out of a mess of ambivalence by subconsciously creating a vivid authority figure who would relieve me of the burden of responsibility for my impulsive act. And once again, maybe he'd have been right. In any event, it worked. Insomnia got to his feet, pleaded another engagement, and slipped out the door. I went back downstairs and back into bed, to sleep soundly for the rest of the night.

When I came home from work the following Friday, David Wells and Mr. Malignon were waiting for me. "I'm glad I had a little time before you got here," David said. "After this box has done some traveling, it always needs adjustment—the bells need to be adjusted. They're set so close together that any little vibrations will leave some in contact with others, and then they won't ring. And I wanted it to sound perfect for you." He smiled. "Did you like the tape?"

"I didn't listen," I said.

"He absolutely refused," said Myra. "*I* listened. But he didn't want to. He said that a tape could never do justice to a box like this—"

"Well, that's true enough," said David.

"—and that he didn't want to hear the music for the first time on a tape. He wanted to hear it as it really sounded."

"First impressions do last," I said. "I didn't want to have a pale copy of that music engraved into wherever it is in my head that those impressions and memories go."

"Well, I can understand that, all right," said David.

He was a huge fellow, six-four or so, with a massive pair of hands and a full mustache. But all his motions were soft and fluid, and his voice was even-toned and mellifluous. A gentle giant, I thought.

We played the box, one tune at a time, stopping between selections, as you might pause between the courses of a particularly fine meal, to fully savor the flavors, and to remark to your companions on the excellence of the preparations. David—and, by extension, Olin—had not exaggerated. In fact, they had, if anything, understated the power of the music in this machine. Considered by itself, the arrangement of the pins on the cylinder was such that the melodies, counter-melodies, and embellishments were exceptional. But the interplay of the voices of the piano and the forte combs, and of the bells, lent a surprising effect to the music; it sounded almost choir-like. Nothing solemn, though; not at all. The music was perky, even saucy. Like a choir, perhaps, on holiday. And as a foundation for all these individual effects was the voice of the music box itself—the voice of this particular maker. Alphonse Malignon's voice. It came across as a background of green silk, infinitely soothing and cool, woven through in geometric patterns by threads of gold and silver, so that the end result was no less than a joyous celebration of metallurgical skills, musical comprehension, acoustical engineering, and artistic vision. Listening to the music, one could not help but see the maker: a round-faced man, clean-shaved, carrying the full weight of wisdom in his dark, gentle eyes. Hands large and calloused; gaze level, but with lines of mild amusement at the corners of his mouth. There is much to be admired in the world, his music seemed to say. Look around yourself. Be properly appreciative. Sing.

The weekend passed too quickly. We took David around Seattle, to tourist spots and tool shops. He and I talked music boxes, and with great patience, he demonstrated to me a number of his restoration techniques. The rapport between us took me by surprise. No matter how well I may think of a person at first impression, it generally takes me a while to warm up to him and to feel comfortable in his presence. But Malignon's initial audition seemed to smash every impediment that might have stood between David and me, and by the end of dinner that night, I felt as though I'd known David and liked him for years. And as the weekend progressed, I gradually came to know and understand a good deal about David's relationship with Elton Norwood.

The story could have been a Greek tragedy. Two young men joined by bonds of a terrible strength, determined to reach a common destination, but disinclined to travel by the same route. United as the Freres de Metatron for the purpose of studying and restoring antique cylinder music boxes, David and Elton were certain that together they could achieve more than either could do alone.

In those early, happy times, Elton and David were held close by more than their passion for music boxes. Both men tended to interpret the world in strongly mystical terms, and so, both held the existence of Cosmic Forces to be a basic tenet of existence. Cosmic Forces—those subtle lines of power which are supposed to give direction to the Universe—are generally regarded by mystics as a representation of divine will: attempts by gods, angels, and other universal guardians to provide guidance to their mortal charges. Thus, one would be well advised to remain aware of and alert to the Forces, since proper alignment with them of your thoughts and activities should facilitate success, happiness, and satisfaction. To ignore the Forces—or even worse, to work consciously against their direction—would be foolish and futile, a senseless waste of energy. Thus, as they labored, Elton and David sought to tune themselves in to the the Forces, that they might always be able to rightfully regard themselves as true brothers of Metatron.

Unfortunately, though, the brothers began to develop divergent readings. They read; they tinkered and they puttered. They talked to music-box historians, and to established restorers. They practiced. They acquired tools. They built machines to suit their own particular needs. With every month, more and more superb music boxes were making that round-trip to Denver, arriving in disarray, and returning home in splendor. Exhilarated by their success, the brothers thought nothing of working sixteen-hour work days when that seemed necessary.

But all that intense mental, emotional, and physical labor generated considerable heat—which appeared to both energize and inspire Elton. His reaction was to turn inward, to work longer and harder hours. At three in the morning, he could be found, sleepless, seeking to break through an incomprehensible restoration problem by immersing himself in a warm bath and trying to establish contact with the maker of a particular box. If only the maker would explain just what he had been about, what he was trying to accomplish—why, then Elton should be able to follow the same line of thinking, and solve the problem. In fact, this approach seems to have been productive: though it might have taken some considerable time, resurrection was a near-certainty for any music box brought into the presence of Elton Norwood.

Unfortunately, the same heat that drove Elton to increasing single-minded effort tended to drive David out the door. In some compartment of his mind, he heard an unceasing nine-voice chorus of disapproval—the entire assemblage of the Muses, endlessly rebuking him for neglecting his sculpture. In addition, David was a skilled fencer, and the Olympics were coming up: if only he could spend enough time practicing, he just *might* make the team. Increasingly, he found it difficult to concentrate all his energies on the music boxes.

Now, at this point, it would have been reasonable for David and Elton to take stock, and restructure their association. And in fact, they did try—but in the process, they saw that the blood they were shedding really *was* thicker than water. It's not all that easy for brothers to redefine their relationship. Elton talked of commitment; David spoke for flexibility. Elton thought that concentration should be paramount; David insisted that diversification would ultimately bring the best results. Elton set industry against dilettantism; David tried to point out that cross-fertilization produces hybrid vigor. Neither could move the other.

To make matters worse, Elton tended to be a definer: when he was satisfied with a technique he'd developed for a particular problem in restoration, he felt that further R and D in that area was both unnecessary and possibly harmful. David, on the other hand, viewed perfection more as an ideal than an actual goal.

As the months went by, the atmosphere in the shop became oppressive. The brothers tried to work on separate schedules, but Elton's fervor and dedication did not leave David enough time to permit him to earn a living. He was reluctant to give up and turn away from the work he loved and the brother with whom he'd shared such glorious triumphs. But finally, it appeared that he had little choice—particularly since the workshop and tools were located in Elton's home.

Who was right? I have no idea, nor, really, do I care. And from this point in the story forward, it doesn't matter.

Another year passed. Elton's reputation grew; he came to be regarded as a miracle worker, capable of giving life to music machines that by any rational criteria should have been pronounced dead. David did what little repair work he felt he could while he pursued his Olympic fencing dream. But when the team was selected, he found himself rated twelfth. Only the first ten made the team. Life was not going well for David, but suddenly it was even worse for Elton. He found himself harboring a fatal disease.

The tragedy drew toward its close. Elton became progressively weaker, and, finally, unable to work. David, distraught, attempted a reconciliation, but Elton would have none of it. At last, Elton was unable to attend to any of his personal needs. David then directed his energies toward making his brother's last days and nights as comfortable as possible.

While he was doing this, he considered the future. Clearly, it was time for another move, but not so clear was the direction. But in any event he'd need to raise some money, and he could think of no reasonable way to do this other than by selling his lovely Malignon music box. He called friends around the country to ask advice. He spoke to Olin Tillotson in Vancouver. Olin said he thought one of the members of his Musical Box Society Chapter might well be interested. David felt mixed emotions which he could not afford. Then, Elton died, and the following evening, David got a call from a fellow in Seattle.

"So, what *are* you going to do," I asked David, as he was getting ready to fly back to Denver.

"Actually, I don't know," he said. Then, he laughed, one of those little chuckles with no humor in it whatever. "I can't help feeling as if I'm at some sort of turning point, but I'm not the least bit sure which way I ought to turn. I'm close to forty, now, and for the first time, there's a girl that I feel serious about— really serious. I think it's time for me to change the way I've been living. But the question is, how? Where do I go from here? Fencing's done; I've had my shot at that. Maybe it was a fool-hardy thing to do, but it was something I wanted to try so badly that I think I can say I *had* to. So, I did. And I guess it's better this way than if I'd never given it a shot. Sculpture? There are things I want to try in sculpture, of course, and if I succeed, there'll be money. But until and unless I do, there's nothing. Right now, what I really wish is that I could go back to the music boxes. I'm good at it—I *know* I am—and the truth is, I've missed them. The last year or so, I've felt as though there's been a huge hole in my life. It's not all that lucrative, considering the time and the work you put in, but it's a living, and it's something I love. I can see myself working at music boxes and sculpture, too. I'm sure there'd be time for both."

"I can see where one of them would feed the other," I said. "They seem like very compatible activities. When you're working on one, the other one shouldn't have any trouble bubbling around at the back of your head, making progress all by itself."

"You under*stand* that," David said.

I thought he looked grateful. "Well, I think I do," I told him.

"I thought you might tell me why don't I get serious for a change. You know—stick to one thing and make it work."

I laughed. Very funny! *I* should tell him to stick to one thing? I, who have never been able to round the edges off the jagged corners of my life, so that they might fit properly together and stop poking me so painfully? I, who was then delivering babies, counseling patients with genetic problems, and administering the day-to-day affairs of both a large hospital obstetrics department and an *in-vitro* fertilization laboratory? I, who at that moment was suffering extravagantly from a major deficiency of hours and minutes to spend at my typewriter, and with my music boxes? I, who had been trying desperately (and without success) to reduce my medical hours, in order to accommodate these other damn things that I wanted to do badly enough that I could say I *had* to do them? *I* should tell him to stick to one thing? Some joke.

"Actually, you *do* sound pretty serious," I said. "At least to me. Maybe you *should* stick to one thing and make it work— but I'm about the last person in the world who'd have the right to tell you that that's the way you ought to do it."

He squeezed my arm. His huge hand was astonishingly gentle. "Thank you," he said, very softly. "I can't tell you how much I appreciate that. Just to hear somebody say that they understand what I'm going through is comforting, and that's something all by itself. I feel…" He drew in a deep breath, and then blew it out hard. "…oh, just completely at sea. Confused. If I at least had those music box tools and supplies, I know exactly what I'd do. But I don't have them. Elton was firm in his conviction that he didn't want to leave the tools to me. I can't really understand the motivation, but that's what he decided, and so there it is. Well, I'm just going to have to figure out something, I guess. At least I'll be starting even, though— thanks to you and Mr. Malignon. But where I go from here…" He held out his palms in a giant shrug.

"I could tell you to just try to follow the Forces," I said.

David didn't say anything. He just put his arms around me and squeezed. This was not the panicky clutch of a drowning man, but a clear expression of calm strength. He was all right, and in one way or another, he was going to stay all right. In just which way, though, I couldn't have said.

Before David left, he made a point of telling me how pleased he was to leave his treasure in my care. "That was one of the things that worried me," he said. "When you offer a box for sale, you just can't know who is going to end up buying it. And I didn't want it to go to the wrong place."

I replied to the effect that he should continue to regard the music box as his. "Money is legal tender," I said. "So, in the legal sense, I do have an interest. But you've invested something a hell of a lot more significant than dollars into it. You can figure that the box is yours, and I'm the legal custodian."

So, here was another music-box bond, this time between a couple of guys, both of whom might have been better off with a little more ability to focus their talents. The only difference between David and me? I'd been fortunate enough to have stumbled into one particular activity through which I could earn a decent living.

But no, wait a minute. That *wasn't* the only difference, was it? Maybe David hadn't yet found a workable way to accommodate his many inclinations, but at least he'd gone out looking. He'd tried things; he'd taken chances. Which of us had shown more courage? Had David's behavior to that point really been less reasonable than mine? Whose future looked more hopeful right then? Which of us had more, and more interesting, possibilities?

"You know," I said to Myra a couple of evenings later. "We really *could* get by on half my income, couldn't we?"

Across the room, the newspaper lowered. I was staring at Gary Cooper across the O. K. Corral, at high noon.

"The kids are through school, and on their own," I contin ued. "It would take some planning—probably even a bit of budgeting—but don't you think we could make expenses on half my pay? If I worked half-time, I really *would* have some reasonable time to attend to my writing and play with my toys."

Myra's jaw relaxed just a bit. "Yes, I guess you would," she said. "But if you did that, you'd better decide you were satisfied with the toys you've got. We could make expenses, yeah, probably. But on half your salary, I can't see there'd be much money for new toys."

I nodded. I'd already thought of that, and I knew it might be a problem. But I told myself I hadn't been enjoying the old toys nearly as much as I thought I ought to.

I began to pursue the possibility of a half-time work schedule. My colleagues and associates at the hospital were not so much opposed as they were frankly mystified. "Aren't you kind of young to retire?" they asked me.

I tried to explain that I was not retiring, or even semi-retiring. "Just a way of restructuring my time, so I can do more of the things I want to do," I said.

"You want to cut your pay in half, so you can sit in front of a typewriter, and putter around with old music boxes?" They scratched their collective head. "Why don't you just enjoy your hobbies at night, and over weekends. Like all of us do."

I talked to David over the phone. "Those people think I'm crazy," I said. "They don't begin to understand, not in the least. You should hear the way some of them actually try to put me down over it."

"I know how that is," said David. "But I think people probably behave that way because somewhere down deep, *they'd* all like to do what you're doing. But they can't bring themselves to it. So, you make them nervous. And then, what they try to do is convince themselves *and* you that you're crazy. That makes them feel more comfortable. You've got to ignore them. Keep faith in yourself." He laughed. "For whatever it's worth, your idea sounds good to me."

David went on to say that Elton Norwood's tools and supplies were now available for purchase. "Probate's a purgatory, nothing less, but now it's over and the tools *are* for sale. I'm checking with banks now to see about arranging a loan."

"With his credit rating, they'll either say no, or hit him with an interest rate that'll set his ears spinning," I told Myra.

A couple of months passed. My half-time work arrangement was all signed and agreed upon. I moved around in a haze of euphoria, interrupted only by an occasional fit of apprehension associated with the notion that my starting date just happened to be April 1. One evening, I came home to find that David had called shortly before. "I've never heard him so excited," Myra said. "He's got an agreement on the sale price, and now all he's got to do is convince the bank, which I suspect may take some doing. But he doesn't seem to mind. He says he's just glad for the chance. He's going at it full tilt."

"I got my bonus check at work today," I said, and pulled an envelope out of my pocket.

"How much?" said Ol' Narrow-Eyes.

"Would you believe within one hundred dollars of what David needs to buy those tools?" I said.

Myra sighed, and then smiled. "Somehow, I'm not altogether shocked," she said. "Well, right now, I guess he needs it more than we do, doesn't he? All right…you know what? We could set him up a loan, say, so that for the first year, he'd just pay interest. That'd give him a chance to get off the ground." "Interesting," I said. "You know what else? We just might have more use for the money a few years from now—right about when he'd be able to pay it back."

"Such a deal," said my wife. "Good for everyone; how can you lose? The Forces strike again. Why don't you give him a call?"

At one-thirty the next morning, I was stretched out on the living room couch, trying to add it all up. I'm a doctor, and doctors are supposed to have no truck with mysticism. And so, all this business about Cosmic Forces was sticking hard in my throat. *Did* I actually believe in the Forces?

I admitted to myself that that was a fair question. Well, all right, then. Did I or didn't I? Was it yes or was it no?

Well, I couldn't exactly say no.

Fine! In that case, was I saying yes?

Well, not exactly....

Now, hold on, I thought. Just stop right there. "Not exactly" means no. "Yes, but..."means no. *Anything* other than yes means no. There's just plain no place here for that genial and tolerant fellow, the gentle skeptic. If it's not yes—yes, with all my heart and soul—then it's no.

But maybe, just maybe...perhaps under all the proper conditions...."

Uh-uh. Maybe is no under any conditions. Now, if I don't believe, why can't I just say no? Just...say...no. Just say it.

Well, but wait, wait a minute. All right, here—here's my answer. I believe. I *do* believe. I believe cosmic forces *do* exist; how's that? Where I'm having trouble is with all those gods, angels, and other universal guardians. Forces with a small f, though—that's fine. Why not? Alone though we all may be in our private worlds, our thoughts and our actions still can and do influence the inhabitants of other worlds. And in turn, we are influenced by the worlds which drift past or circle around our own. These worlds extend to affect us both vertically from the past, and horizontally from the present. And since there have existed multiple billions of human lives from the beginning of time, these reciprocal influences—call them forces, if you'd like—can become quite dense and complex. They are part of nature—and as such, they are neutral. They don't know we exist, let alone care whether we use them wisely or foolishly. Whether they come to appear benign or malevolent will depend in great part on how well *we* read *them*. It's also up to us to determine the manner in which the force lines extend into the future—to designate what sorts of forces will present themselves to our descendants.

As I thought of the forces in this respect, I was put in mind of an old golf teacher, seventy if he was a day, who once watched me practically throw my spine out of alignment as I dribbled shot after futile, frustrating shot off the tee. "You're going at it all wrong," the old guy said. "Look: you're not letting the club do the work. You think you gotta do it all yourself. Do like this." And he took my driver out of my hand, stepped up to the tee, addressed the ball, took the most casual-looking swing I'd ever seen in my life, and walloped the ball 225 yards straight down the middle of the fairway. "See," he said, stepping away, and handing me back my club. "*That's* a golf shot. You gotta just help the club out. Get it where it needs to go. Once it's there, *it* knows what the hell to do."

I thought about the events of the past several weeks. There was David Wells, given the second chance he so desperately wanted, and the opportunity all the more dear to him for the price he needed to pay for it. And like David's slightly-distorted mirror image, there *I* was, paying no less dearly for my own desperately-wanted second chance. In the process, we had both found the sympathetic and helpful friend one always wishes for at these critical moments. And finally, the custodianship of an extraordinary music box, a machine even more special now than it ever was before, had been resolved in a manner that left both of us satisfied and deeply grateful.

Was all this the forces at work or at play? Were we, all of us, moving in such finely-tuned harmony with those mysterious lines of universal interpersonal persuasion that in the last analysis a man's love for his brother had managed to gain the upper hand over his anger, such that a determination to permanently slam closed the doors to the home of Metatron was transformed into a beneficent gift?

Or was it all no more than an overactive imagination acting upon a series of coincidences, a run of those random occurrences that we all take for granted in the course of our everyday living? The sort of thing that happens to all of us all the time, but that a writer can never use in a story.

No doubt, this would be the opinion of that consulting psychiatrist. And no question, that would be one way to look at it.

But there's another way. Remember the *deus ex machina* of the ancient theater, the god who would step out of a box, and with a casual wave of his hand immediately resolve the dramatic conflict? Well, a day rarely passes in our own lives that we don't open one sort of box or another and find a god blinking up at us. But whether in a play, a novel, or our own lives, we discount it. It's too pat, too unbelievable. It didn't really happen. That sort of thing went out with the ancient Greeks. We call ourselves sophisticated, but all that really comes down to is that we lack the capacity to appreciate the miracle in the commonplace. By definition, miracles lie outside the domain of Reason. Either you believe in miracles or you don't. No maybes. And there's Logic, always lying in wait, eternally ready to try to convince us that our senses must be mistaken. No, nothing there, not really. Just probability playing its silly games again. Just a coincidence.

Finally, here, at the end of the story, what shall we say of Elton Norwood? Well, toward the end of the services on Yom Kippur, the Hebrew Day of Atonement, as the congregants ask that their sins be forgiven, they pray that a light may shine forth on the morning of their deaths, that from their graves may sprout not the barren thistle, but the fragrant myrtle. And so, now, in terms of the restoration of damaged lives no less than of damaged music boxes, Elton's light continues to shine brilliantly, a proper memorial to his driven, searching spirit, and a clear indication of how strong the forces can be when they're applied with care, and wisdom, and humane generosity. As to the question of from whom or where that strength derives, that's a story for another time, and probably another teller.

The Greatest Music Box in the World

My friend Leroy doesn't have the slightest interest in mechanical music. In fact, he thinks I'm a prize nut case for all the time and energy I put into my music boxes. He tells me that my behavior makes him want to believe in God. "I only hope that some day you're going to have to answer to *somebody* for all of this wasted time," he's forever muttering at me.

Leroy's passion is computers. He was one of these high-school kids who read all about Univac, and then spent entire weekends in the attic, sticking silicon chips together with lengths of wire. He majored in math in college, and then got into one of the new computer science graduate programs. Now, he's a department chairman, a very important and well-respected man in his field. He logs more air time than Kissinger, zipping around the world to go to conferences and give talks. As far as Leroy is concerned, the entire story of World Civilization is no more than a preamble, the tedious but obligatory eons of preparation for the Great Computer Era. In Leroy's book, the beginning of modern history was signaled by the founding of Sperry Rand.

I first met Leroy six years ago, when I was called in to attend to his wife during a dreadfully complicated pregnancy. Fortunately, the outcome was good. A couple of years later, they tried for a second baby, and once again, after considerable *sturmen und drangen*, they came up winners. Throughout the entire business, as sick as Leroy's wife got, dealing with Leroy himself remained the most difficult issue. Plainly put, the man was impossible. At every step along the way, he was exasperated to fidgets by my inability to offer him unequivocal predictions as to what was going to happen next. Computer-persons tend to be like that; so do accountants and engineers. In their minds, two and two always seem to add up to four. And if a particular circuit is not working properly, why then you just plain go in and rewire it. These people don't seem to appreciate that a human machine is perfectly capable of adding two to two, and spitting out six and seven-eighths whenever it darned well pleases. In medicine, it may be impossible, even in retrospect, to identify which circuit was the mischievous one.

So, there gradually arose between Leroy and me an odd sort of friendship, based, I think, upon a perverse sort of fascination over the differences between us. Certainly, there was mutual respect: we accepted both the sincerity and the skills of the other, but after each knock-down, drag-out session in my office, we'd part in thorough frustration, as much with ourselves as with the other. How *could* the other be so obtuse? In the way that some men go to the gym together to work out, we started to go (with our wives) to dinner. Which our wives could not understand. Why would the two of us want to go out and give each other pains in the stomach? Well, it wasn't really that we wanted to. It just always seemed to work out that way.

Try to imagine, then, how I felt one afternoon when Leroy called me to say that he had a music box he thought I'd like to hear, and that I should come over to his house. My response was to ask him whether he was kidding.

"What do you mean, kidding?" Leroy said. "That's the thanks I get, huh? I go to the trouble to find you a nice music box, and all you can do is ask am I kidding?"

"Don't get huffy, Leroy," I said. "Listen: you've got to admit, this isn't exactly something I'd have expected from you."

"So, is that *my* problem?" Leroy snapped. "Look, I'm just trying for once to talk to you in your own language. You do have to talk to people in their own language, don't you? Even crazy people." He paused, and then added, "*Especially* crazy people."

"Okay," I said. "All right; stop. Consider me properly chastened. I'll give you the benefit of the doubt. See you right after work."

Leroy met me at the door, and greeted me, as he always did, with that little smile which I call his physiognomy of sardonic bemusement. He watched, as I swept my gaze around the hallway and into the living room behind. "The collector salivates without control or remorse," Leroy said. "Come on. Your treasure is back in my den."

He might as well have said his cave, or his lair. I call the place The Electronic Jungle, and it's a harsh, scary land, full of danger for the innocent and uninitiated. You have to watch your step with great care, lest some malevolent wire or cable grab you by the ankle and throw you to the ground, to be devoured by one of the anthropophagous computers or printers. From floor to ceiling on all sides, the self-multiplying reference books and cassette monsters perch on their shelves, ready at the slightest bump to descend upon you with full fury, knocking you unconscious and rendering you easy prey to those innocent-appearing mounds of their floor-dwelling brethren. And always, in the background, there's that ominous hum, the silicon-sound that summons the attention of the entire hideous band of electronic denizens. Full alert, it proclaims. Nonbeliever approaching.

I looked around the room as bravely as I dared, but still I saw no music box. Leroy, moving easily and without apparent fear, picked up a cassette from his desk and held it out toward me. "Here it is," he said. "Are you ready for the treat of your life?"

"It's . . . just a tape?" I said.

"Well, sure," said Leroy. "What did you think — the owner was going to offer to *give* me the actual box to take home with me? Besides, even if he had, I couldn't have done it; I'd have needed a moving van and four strong men. I thought you'd be glad that I at least persuaded him to let me make a recording."

"Okay, Leroy, all right," I said, and waved my hand in a stop signal. "I'm sorry. Go ahead and play the tape. I want to hear it."

He shook the cassette out of its plastic cover, and held it up like a trophy. "Listen to it, and then tell me what you think," he said.

"I'll bet you're not gonna be disappointed. Go on, now. Sit down and listen."

The only chair in the room was Leroy's, at Control Central, and there was not a patch of clear floor anyplace that was anywhere near large enough for me to consider lowering myself on to. Danger everywhere. "It's all right," I said. "I'll stand up."

Leroy's enthusiastic words notwithstanding, I felt disappointed in anticipation as he slipped the cassette into the tape deck. Music boxes are notoriously difficult to record properly, and even under the best circumstances, a tape does not come near to doing justice to the sound of the machine. I felt as if I'd been invited to hear a performance by a world-class singer, only to be told that it would be no more than a quickly-arranged sound recording.

As the music began to emerge from Leroy's weirdly-shaped, giant, plate-like speakers, though, I forgot all about those feelings, and in a hurry. What I was listening to were the opening phrases of Beethoven's Fifth Symphony — obviously being played by a music box. But what a music box! In a dim way, I realized that I was fortunate, having heard as many music box recordings as I had, together with live performances from the same machines. So now, I was able to make proper allowance, and by a process of mental transposition, I could hear the music in my mind quite as I felt it would have sounded had the music box itself been there before me. The bass was a golden weaving, all thick, loosely-arrayed rope-like strands, and this was overlaid by a kaleidoscopic treble of vibrant blues, reds, and greens. The treble was in perpetual motion, constantly shifting and restructuring, as though desperately seeking a home for itself. The first three chords of the music were perfect -- clear and sharp — and the fourth, the knock of fate, terminated in a lovely arpeggio which slid imperceptibly into a rapidly-rising and falling sequence where the notes came to blend into a gossamer glissando. When this effect finally faded, it left an amber-pink glow, which in turn shimmered into momentary silence. And then, the entire length of the comb took over, the mid-section singing a glorious melody line, while the bass beneath wove a perfectly-balanced golden support. Meanwhile the extreme treble played an accompaniment of green trills, wavy orange runs, and occasional emphasis notes of the purest scarlet. Here and there, I could pick out subtle, captivating mandolin-like effects.

"I don't be*lieve* this," I said to Leroy.

"Shh. Be quiet." Leroy held his finger to his lips. "Just listen, would you. After it's done, I want to hear what you think of it."

I looked at the floor near my feet, and then, drawing up my courage, I gave a stack of computer magazines a shove with the side of my shoe. Then, I sat down, leaned back against the bookcase, and listened.

I was certain that I was hearing something unprecedented in music-box history. Without a pause, the recording went through the entire first movement of the Beethoven Fifth, the whole 12 minutes fully as magnificent as the opening bars had been. Then, there was a familiar click, signalling the shutting off of the cylinder at the end of play, and after that, a pause.

"They're changing the barrel now," Leroy said.

"Cylinder," I corrected. "Mechanical organs have barrels. Music boxes have cylinders."

"Whatever you call it." Leroy smirked.

I ignored the bait. Never mind that Leroy would throw a fit whenever somebody referred to a computer, rather than its software, as a word processor. I wanted no arguments right then. I heard a second click, that of the start lever being pushed. The second movement was beginning.

The experience was disorienting. To my knowledge, nothing like a full symphony had ever been arranged for a music box, nor did cylinder machine programs feature much music at all by Beethoven. The voice of the cylinder music box presents itself as more compatible with the Austrian spice and sugar of Mozart and the Strausses, or the warm Italian sun of Verdi and Rossini, than with the wild and ponderous musical Teutonisms of Beethoven. Nonetheless, no one would have questioned the authorship of this music. Each phrase was a clear utterance from the soul of Beethoven, and no one else. And though the music was in no way emasculated or even sanitized, it occurred to me that the voice of this particular machine had given expression to a previously-unrecognized dimension of the composer's speech, an aspect perhaps previously heard only by Beethoven himself. For the first time, I could appreciate, mixed through the early, stormy passages of the Fifth Symphony, the clear promise of the joyous reconciliation and redemption to be spoken of openly in the chorale section of the Ninth.

I leaned back full against the bookcase, stretched my legs out straight in front of me, and listened to the third, and then the fourth, movement. I was concerned that the instrument might be unequal to the job of transmitting the power and the passion of the coda, and this was not a performance that I wanted to hear go out with a whisper. But I needn't have worried. The coda proved to be no more a problem for this astonishing music box than had been the apparently-uncongenial opening measures: as delicate as was the voice of the performer, it still seemed to possess a limitless reserve of fire. As the music drew to the close, great booming golden chords flew from the bass teeth, while a psychedelic rainbow of intertwined embellishments coursed up and down huge segments of the remainder of the comb, setting off parallel waves of goose flesh along my spine.

As the amber luminescence of the last notes faded out, Leroy reached up to shut off the tape player. He grinned. "It was pretty good, wasn't it?" he said.

I swallowed. "'Pretty good' is hardly the word for it," I said. I realized that my legs were painfully stiff, and I drew them up to my chest, and stretched. "Leroy . . ."

"Yeah, Larry?"

He looked like a superannuated Eagle Scout. Bright eyes, bright cheeks. "Leroy," I repeated. "You said they changed the cylinder after each movement. Isn't that right?"

"Yeah. So ?"

"So there were four cylinders, altogether?"

"For the Beethoven symphony, yes."

I didn't think it was possible, but my excitement went up another notch. "That's what I was getting at," I said. "There were more cylinders, then?"

"Oh, sure," Leroy answered. "A load of them. They were piled up under the table, in wooden boxes. Sort of like orange crates."

"What was *on* them?" I shouted. "What kind of music, I mean?"

Leroy shrugged. "Oh . . . I don't know," he said. "Pretty much the same stuff. Other symphonies. That sort of thing."

"How many?"

"Well, I don't *know*, Larry," Leroy said. "I just didn't look. I mean, I didn't realize that was important. I thought I did pretty well, just getting you this recording."

"You did, Leroy," I said. "You did great. That's the most wonderful music box I've ever heard."

"Really?" Leroy looked amused. "*The* greatest?"

"Oh, yes," I said. "Definitely. Listen, Leroy. There's something here that's truly extraordinary — something almost supernatural. It's altogether beyond a well-crafted machine that plays beautiful two-minute musical arrangements. You just don't find symphonic music by Romantic composers on cylinder music boxes; the voice is all wrong for the material. You'd think it would come across, say, like Bing Crosby singing *Vesti la giubba*. But whoever designed that machine and arranged its music must have had a unique musical mind. He's not only got Bing singing opera, he's got him singing it in a whole new way that's absolutely wonderful. He heard something in Bing Crosby's voice that nobody else knew was there, and I don't know how, but he brought it out and took full advantage of it. And that literally gave a whole new dimension to the music. You listened to it! Have you ever heard Beethoven say as much, and say it so beautifully? I mean in *any* performance of *any* symphony?"

Leroy turned his physiognomy of sardonic bemusement back on –- which didn't surprise me in the least. He enjoyed making fun of me for the way I "heard voices" when I listened to music boxes. "Isn't that a symptom of schizophrenia, Doctor?" he would ask me. "Hearing voices, I mean. Auditory hallucinations, isn't that what they're called? I thought your profession treated people like that with strong medications, and locked them up in safe places." As far as Leroy was concerned, music boxes played music, and not very impressive music, either. "For the life of me, I can't understand how you can get so worked up over them," he'd say. "Or waste all that time fooling with them. I mean, if you like music that much, why don't you just go to the symphony? Or the opera? Buy a good CD player. My God, I think I'd go out of my gourd, listening the way you do to that tinkly, tinkly, crap for hours on end."

I decided to stay clear of confrontation. No arguments, not right then. This was prioritizing time, and I knew very clearly what was Number One in my mind. "Leroy," I said. "I need to hear that machine."

Leroy's smile melted into confusion. "What do you mean, you need to 'hear that machine?'" he said. "You just heard it."

"No, no, Leroy. I mean, hear it in person. In the flesh. The actual machine. I want to hear that music as it's really being played –- and then, I want to hear the other cylinders, too."

"You can't," Leroy almost snapped.

"What do you mean, I can't? Why not?"

"Because . . . well, because the guy who owns it is a little funny –- even for a music box collector," Leroy said. "He's not just going to let you walk in and listen."

"Sure he will," I said. "I get visitors all the time, collectors from all over the country and around the world. We visit back and forth. Just about any collector would let another collector hear his machines."

"Well, he doesn't live around here," said Leroy.

"That much I knew," I snapped back at him. "If he did, I'd know him — especially if he had a music box anything like this one. But he did let you in, didn't he? So, I have to figure he'd let me in, too. Especially if you tell him I'm your friend."

"I'm not so sure about that," Leroy muttered.

"Come on, Leroy," I barked. "Did you really think you were going to play that tape for me, and I'd just listen to it and say thank you, that was great, and that would be the end of it? You told me how great this music box was —"

"Yeah, for a music box," Leroy interrupted. "It was a nice music box, actually. It had a pretty case, nice wood, with all sorts of fancy metal inlay on the lid. And it sat up on a matching table that was really very attractive. I did think its sound was quite good –- at least I guessed it would be to a person who liked music boxes. So, I thought of you, and I made a recording. And now, for thanks, you're going to nag me to death."

"You're absolutely right about that, Leroy," I said. "I'll hound you to the grave and beyond, if I have to. Now, look. You just got back from Kansas City. You went to a computer meeting there. So, this collector must be a computer person, or at least a friend of a computer person, who lives out that way. Isn't that right?"

"Your deductive powers astonish me, Doctor Watson!" Leroy grinned. "All right –- but wait a minute. Am I really to believe that you would just jump onto a plane and zip out to Kansas City? Just like that? To hear a music box? Why, you'd be even crazier than I thought."

"I doubt that's possible," I said. "And yes, you are to believe it. Why not? I fly to a lot of places to hear music boxes, or to buy them. But who are you to say that's crazy? You spend more time on airplanes going to and from computer meetings than you do at home."

"That's my *work*," Leroy howled.

"Oh!" I shouted back. "That's your *work*! You couldn't possibly stay here in Seattle and work on computers, could you? People are forcing you to fly to New York, and London, and Tokyo. They put you onto planes at gunpoint. Listen, Leroy: spare me the pious judgements, would you please. Just get me an invitation to hear that music box. And don't tell me you can't. If I have to, I'll call you at night. I'll keep waking you up every two hours until you do it."

"I'll disconnect my phone," Leroy said.

"I'll throw stones at your bedroom window," I shot back.

Leroy looked hard at me. "I believe you would, you goddamn Bedlamite," he said.

"You believe correctly,' I said.

He sighed. "I'll get back to you."

"Good," I said. "And oh, by the way. Thanks for making me that tape. I appreciate it; I really do."

"Thank me no thanks," said Leroy. "You do something nice for a person, and you see what happens. I swear, they ought to lock guys like you up where they won't do anybody any harm.

Two days later, Leroy called back. It wasn't easy, he told me, but he'd talked to his associate, the man who owned the wonderful music box. He told the man that I might never again sleep or know a moment's peace if I were not to hear that stupid machine play. And the sooner the better, otherwise he — Leroy — might also never again sleep or know a moment's peace. So, the man had agreed to my visit. "You can fly out Saturday morning," Leroy said. "I hope that'll be soon enough for you."

"It's fine," I told him. "Better than I expected, in fact. You thought you were being funny, didn't you, with that line about me never sleeping again? Well, you weren't. Just for the record."

That's normal collector behavior. For two full nights, now, ever since I'd heard Leroy's recording, I'd thrashed around in bed, trying to find a position which might shut out that incredible sound and sight. But of course, there was no such position. Any way I arranged myself, the box played on and on.

Larry trudged up to the dark living room,
and the box played on.
He sat in his chair and he tore at his hair,
and the box played on.
And his head was so loaded, it damn near exploded:
he set off the burglar alarm.
His wife and the cops were just madder than hops,
and the box played on.

Toward morning, I'd doze off, but then, as the clock-radio began to play, the newscast was instantly drowned out by the green and the gold of Beethoven's Fifth Symphony.

I thought Leroy would follow my confession with a juicy wisecrack, but to my surprise, he didn't take the bait. "You can take the 8:30 flight out of Sea-Tac," he said. It gets to Kansas City at 12:05. The owner of the box will meet you at the gate. If that's not convenient for you, I'll have to call him back."

"Hell, no," I roared. "Don't even *think* of calling him back. I'm free the weekend; I'll go at his convenience. "What's the flight number?"

"Oh . . . United, Number 87," said Leroy. And his name is Bill. Bill Gasperette."

By the time Flight 87 hit the air, my gizzard was a mixmaster running amuck, thoroughly out of control. I was on my way to hear probably the greatest music box in the world. What if it didn't live up to expectations? Not likely, I told myself, and even if it did happen, the fault would probably be mine -- the result of four days of intense recollection, producing expectations unrealistic by any standard. Another thing . . . could the box possibly be for sale? Or might it be obtained by way of a trade? The present owner simply might not have an ear for cylinder music boxes. "Yeah," he might say, "I know it's a nice one, all right, but give me a good Regina any time." And if he did, I would. On the spot.

Well, that would be nice — but to listen to this box through its entire repertoire was my primary goal, and that would be sufficient. I thought about what I might hear in the voice of the arranger, over the course of thirty, or maybe forty, cylinders. And if the box's owner did have a properly-tuned ear for cylinder machines, what might we discover as we listened together to the music? I would check the details of construction of the box; I'd check for clues as to the maker. Maybe the owner would tell me where he'd managed to find this treasure.

I knew that whatever were to happen over this weekend, I would be bringing something of great value home with me on the return flight. Maybe it would be a music box; maybe the beginnings of a deep and valuable friendship. Maybe knowledge; maybe understanding. Or any combination of the above. And any of them worth at least the price of the fare, and the time spent. Why couldn't Leroy see that? Why couldn't he realize that there was more to collecting than simply filling up your home with objects? People who do that are really not collectors. They're pack rats — they acquire and they hoard. They simply need to have, and to store away; it's a form of miserly behavior where the stinginess and avarice are affixed to objects, rather than to money. Properly done, collecting can be the vehicle for expression of a major philanthropic passion. At the same time that I was twitching with anticipatory excitement for myself, I felt profoundly sorry for Leroy.

Bill Gasperette picked me right out as I came through the line into the terminal, but I'd never have recognized him. He was a young man, not more than thirty-five, with uncombed, shaggy hair, and thick glasses that magnified and transmitted the light from his brown eyes to a disconcerting degree of intensity. He was wearing a wrinkled white shirt, open-necked, and a pair of rumpled jeans with a threadbare patch on the right knee. None of this put me off, by the way. I've long since stopped being astonished when a man who looks one step removed from a bed at the local mission house digs into his pocket at an auction and casually pulls out a roll of hundred-dollar bills to pay off a multi-thousand-dollar tab. Bill was all good cheer, grinning and chuckling; he pumped my hand and told me that any friend of Leroy's was a friend of his. Then, he said that he bet I was real anxious, now, wasn't I, to hear this music box.

Bill's manner was that of the social maladroit. He was the kid we all knew in high school and college, the one with the IQ of 180, straight A's, and the full scholarship to M.I.T. The one who said "Aw, shucks," when a girl approached him to talk, and who was always scratching himself at parties and dinners. The one who could never manage to hold up his end of any kind of conversation, because his mind was bursting with dancing numbers or words. Or musical notes.

It fit. The guy was probably a computer whiz, which explained his connection to Leroy. While earning his living at one sort of terminal or another, he had fallen under the spell of music boxes — you tell me just why it happens to any of us — and then, in the course of his everyday affairs, he'd happened to stumble over this exceptional machine. He'd said, "Well, looky here!" and then had carted the thing home. Who says God doesn't temper winds to shorn lambs? And of course, this was not the sort of guy who would belong to any of the musical box societies, so no one would ever have heard about his treasure. Not till he'd happened to mention it to Leroy, during a break in one of their computer conversations.

I told Bill I was very happy to meet him, and that I was grateful for his hospitality. And yes, I was real anxious to hear this music box.

"Well, I'll take you right over and play it for you." He laughed.

He led me through the parking lot to a little gray Toyota pickup. I tossed my suitcase into the back, and as I got in, Bill reached up to the dashboard, and handed me an envelope. "For you," he said. "It's from Leroy. He told me on the phone I should be sure and give it to you soon as you come." Again, Bill laughed, that uneasy chuckle misfits use to cover their discomfort at being forced out of their solitary thought patterns. "That Leroy! You just never do know what he's about, do you?"

No, I thought. I don't. I looked at the envelope. It was postmarked Thursday, the same day Leroy had called to tell me of the arrangements. On the lower left was an overnight express sticker.

I know I shrugged as I tore the envelope open. By now, Bill had backed out of the parking space, and was driving slowly up the service road toward the highway. As soon as I unfolded the typewritten letter, I saw that it was in fact intended for me. "Dear Lunatic," read Leroy's salutation,

Whatever you do, just go along with Bill. Just listen and keep your mouth shut. No matter what he says, or what happens, don't get sore at him, and don't start yelling. Don't get into any discussions, and don't make any stupid accusations. Be sure to keep smiling, and be nice. Then, after you get back, we can talk.

Have fun.

Love and kisses,

Leroy

I read through it twice, and then folded it quickly and stuffed it back inside the envelope. I looked sidewise at Bill; he seemed not the least interested in the letter. His face was relaxed as he drove along the interstate toward Kansas City. Was he one of these crazies who's perfectly fine until somebody challenges him — or until he *thinks* somebody's challenging him? And then he goes bananas; starts swinging bottles and brandishing fireplace andirons? Could be. That would also explain why no one had ever seen or heard this super music box, and it would also explain why Leroy was so reluctant to call him on my behalf. And why his very first remark was to the effect that if I was a friend of Leroy's, I must be okay. But why hadn't Leroy just told me all this on the phone?

I decided to stop asking questions I couldn't possibly answer. In fact, I decided to stop asking questions altogether. I was going to hear a spectacular music box, and whatever might follow on that would be fine. I spent the rest of the ride telling Bill about some of my own music machines. He just kept grinning, and saying that my music boxes sounded like they'd be awful nice, and maybe some day, he could get to hear them. Though I did harbor a few reservations, I kept them very private, and told him I thought that would be nice.

Bill pulled up in front of a low, whitewashed building in a commercial part of town, all small businesses and little restaurants. I thought he was stopping to pick up some bread or club soda, but he grinned again, gestured at the building, and said, Well, here we were.

"This is where you *live*?" I said

Too late, I remembered Leroy's letter. I wanted to bite my tongue. Fortunately, though, Bill just laughed. "Well, no," he said. "Why would I be livin' here? But you *did* want to hear that music box, didn't you?"

"Oh, absolutely," I said, very quickly. "Yes. I can't wait, in fact."

"Well, o-*kay*!" Bill slapped his leg. "Let's go on in, then."

We were two steps inside before he turned on the light. The place was a horror, worse even than Leroy's den. A single room filled the entire building, and it was crammed with electronic equipment. Each piece seemed to be connected to at least one other by a tangle of wires more complex than the Gordian knot. There was a keyboard at each corner of the compass. Microphones, angular and oddly dysmorphic, regarded me balefully with their single unblinking eyes. Floor-to-ceiling shelves projected at right angles from three of the four walls; they were loaded with cassettes, CD's, LP records, and sheet music. At the far corner of the room, a computer console was holding court, dispensing mandates via wire linkages to the eight or ten rectangular machines scattered here and there around the room. God only knew what these things were . . . but I didn't have a clue. My only certainty was that none of them was a music box.

"Y' ready to hear it?" Bill shouted. He was holding up a floppy disk, waving it like a trophy.

I came perilously close to saying I'd already heard that particular it, but this time, I remembered my warning, and simply nodded. Bill slid the disk into his computer, and pushed a button. Immediately, the room filled with the first notes of Beethoven's Fifth Symphony.

All at once, I understood. This *was* the original. Someone — probably my host here — had somehow and for some reason managed to coax a surprisingly good impersonation of a music-box out of a computer. My disappointment was deep, but at the same time, it was tempered by curiosity. Why in hell had I been induced to fly out to Kansas City, just to listen to a fake — a synthesized mechanical music performance? Oh yes, I was more than willing to admit, the feat was impressive. True, the genuine tonal qualities of a fine cylinder music box had really not been achieved: what I had at first hearing attributed to the shortcomings of a tape recording, I could now recognize as some of the more minor manifestations of "computer music". But still, the performance was good enough to have led me into making this mistake, and that spoke considerably for the abilities of the perpetrators.

Even more interesting, I realized that if I focused on an image of the "real" music box which was supposed to have produced the recording, all the sound colors instantly intensified. The experience then became fully that of the first audition, all my emotions recapitulating those which had come over me at Leroy's. As the symphony progressed, I found that by playing with my mental viewpoint, I could produce a most interesting alternating visual pattern: the actual rainbow, then a photograph. Full engagement of senses and emotions, then an intellectual appreciation of a performance. Being, then doing. Living, then watching. By the end of the music, I was exhausted. Sweat was rolling down behind my ears.

Bill laughed as he pushed another button on the computer. "Not bad for a first try, huh?" he said. "Betcha want to know just how I did it now, right?"

"Oh, yes," I said, swallowing. "Absolutely. Don't leave anything out."

"Well!" Bill drew in a deep breath, then blew it out. "When Leroy told me what it was you were after, I knew it wasn't gonna be a piece of cake. But I figured it could be done. Just a matter of trial and error . . ."

Then, he proceeded to tell me all about his trials and his errors, such as they had been. By comparison, a recounting of the details of a piece of brain surgery would have been mundane. He'd gotten the name of a local collector, and had gone to listen to some of the collector's music boxes. He recorded the boxes. He took the recordings back to his studio, and fed the poor things to his computer. He let the beast digest the material for a while, and then he and the computer entered into earnest discourse. The computer returned him an analysis of the sound qualities of the various music boxes, which material he fed to something called a sampling synthesizer. This new collaborator was then able to help him generate notes of reasonably-appropriate timbre; it was on this part of the work that he spent most of his time. Designating proper timbre remains the weak point of any computer-generated music, but Bill got it as close as he could. Then, he added in just enough background noise to disguise the fact that the timbre simply could not be got perfectly right, and also to create verisimilitude for a "casual" tape recording. And at that point, having created a bank of the proper notes over three and a half octaves, it was simply a matter of setting them into the correct arrangement. I say simply. Actually, Bill explained, it had taken Leroy and him the better part of four full nights during the conference, and then three entire days and nights after the end of the meeting.

I tried to pretend I understood. It seemed clear that Bill thought I was able to follow the details of his explanation, and I was being very careful not to offend him. Whether Leroy had told him I was also a computer maven, perhaps in order to gain me entree, or whether Bill was just one of those very bright people who find it impossible to imagine that there actually exist persons with limited computer comprehension, I had no idea. But if he wanted to believe I was following his every fine point, and eagerly awaiting the next, I did not wish to disabuse him of the notion. I just kept nodding my head, and at what seemed like the proper intervals, saying, "Yup", or "Uh-huh", or "Oh . . . sure!"

My computer stupidity notwithstanding, I was surprised to find myself actually interested in Bill's story — very much so, in fact. Imagine being able to create a very believable music-box sound, and then to arrange a musical performance that would have been unattainable on a genuine machine. It was ingenious, and the degree of its success had been limited by no more than a technical boundary — a boundary certain to disappear in the not-distant future.

"But you know what really got me interested?" Bill continued.

I braced myself for another onslaught of Killer Technology Verbiage.

"It was Leroy," Bill said. "I mean, I just couldn't get over what he did. How he worked at that arrangement. And how good it came out."

"What do you mean?" I asked.

"Well, what I said," said Bill. "About Leroy. I figured it was me who was gonna have to do the arrangement — I mean, I'm the musician, right? But Leroy had the manuscript for the symphony right with him when he got here, and he'd been working on it already. He told me that he had to do that part because he knew more about the music boxes than I did, 'cause of all of yours that he'd been listening to. So he'd know better how you'd want it to sound. He said he could already hear the music in his head. All he wanted me to do was help him with the technical part of it, to put it all together. And more than once, when I saw what he was up to, I thought, Oh no; this is gonna sound absolutely *awful!* But it never did, not once. I'll tell you, I just wouldn't have believed a person could make the Beethoven Fifth sound anything *like* that. But what do *you* think? Did we do okay?"

I nodded my head firmly, and said, "Yes. Absolutely. In fact, you exceeded my expectations."

Bill's goggly eyes beamed joy at me through the coke-bottle lenses.

"Well, where do we go from here, then?" said Bill.

"I'll let you know," I told him. First, I'll have to talk to Leroy.

I thought Leroy looked just a bit ill at ease when I walked in on him at his university office. He recovered quickly, though, and flashed sardonic bemusement into my eyes. "Well," he said. "The globe-trotting hallucinator is home, I see. Did you have a good trip?"

"Actually, yes," I said. "Very useful. And very interesting."

"Oh, really?" Leroy swiveled his chair to face me directly. "Exactly what was so useful and so interesting about flying halfway across the country to listen to a voice that never existed, except in the larynx of a computer? Now, are you ready to admit just how foolish an unleashed imagination can make a man look?"

"One thing first, Leroy?" I said. "Just tell me whether Bill was in on this joke, too."

Leroy laughed, and said, "What, are you kidding? No, of course not. I just told him you were a musician of sorts, with a particular interest in music boxes. You'd been talking to me about trying to find out whether computers could be used to take music box sounds one step further. And I told you that if anyone could do it, Bill could, and that I'd make a tape with him at the meeting. Then, if you thought the results were promising, you might want to take the work even further. Okay?"

"Yeah, just fine," I said. "Because that's exactly what happened."

Leroy's physiognomy sagged into an adenoidal stare.

"That's right," I said. "You knew what I wanted even better than I knew myself. That *was* a very impressive tape, Leroy — it was impressive when I thought it came from a music box, and it was even more impressive when I found out what it really was. Because for all the time I've spent listening to those voices that you're so fond of making fun of, until now, I've never even thought about the possibility of speaking, myself. I mean, I wasn't about to try to build a music box from scratch. But this is wonderful: what an opportunity! I am going to work some more with Bill. I want to see how much further he can help me take this work."

"What are you talking about?" Leroy snapped. The skin on his face was as tight as the tone of his voice. "You don't know anything about computers."

"Yes I do," I said. "I know what they can do for me, because now you've shown me. I know someone who can help me work with them, because you introduced us. Sure, I've got a lot to learn, but so what? I'll read what I need to, and I'll practice. And I'll talk to Bill."

"That's preposterous," Leroy snorted. "The World Champion Computer Idiot is going to do *what*? Tell me: do you remember them warning you to put on an oxygen mask on the flight home?"

"I know at least as much about computers as you do about music," I said.

"What does what I know about music have to do with anything?" said Leroy.

"Bill told me who put that Beethoven arrangement together," I said. "You were right, actually: you did have to do it yourself, because you *were* the one who knew what I wanted to hear. But you were wrong when you said I went flying across the country to hear the voice of a computer. That was no computer's voice, Leroy — not any more than the voice of a music box is the voice of the mechanism. It's the arranger's voice — it's *always* the voice of the arranger. Whether it's François Nicole, David Lecoultre . . . or you, Leroy. That was *your* voice I heard on that tape. Your voice and your music."

Leroy backed away from me. "You *are* crazy, you know that?" He was up out of his chair, now, and shouting. "You're a Grade A fruitcake. Listen, you damn fool. That was a fraud, pure and simple. Do I have to draw you a diagram? I was playing a trick on you. Just a trick; that's all it was."

I shook my head. "Uh-uh. People don't work a whole week, all day and through the night, on just a little trick. If there's a joke, it's on you. You thought you were saying one thing, but you were really saying something entirely different. You know what, Leroy? You really ought to try listening to your own voice while you're talking. You just might be absolutely amazed."

Which ended the interview. Leroy muttered something about having to go teach a class, which may or may not have been true. And since then, whenever I've tried to open the subject again, he shuts me off with a remark to the effect that he's not in the habit of talking to walls.

So, I talk to Bill Gasperette instead. We spend time on the phone; we send disks and tapes back and forth. I've been working on an arrangement of the Beethoven Ninth Symphony, and he's seeing what he can do to improve the quality of the timbre. When we've both gotten a little farther, I'll fly back out to K. C. and we'll get down to some actual taping. If it's good enough, I'll bring back a copy to play for Leroy.

After all, you really should try to talk to a person in his own language.

෴

There Oughta Be a Law

he sight of a fine old music box in non-working condition sends my heart flying forward to drum a refrain of hopeful anticipation against my breastbone. Maybe I can pick up a great machine for my collection, and at a bargain price — and then, on top of that, have the pleasure of restoring the voice and appearance of the singer. Who could ask for anything more?

Before I ever permit my heart to fly too far or for too long, though, I'm careful to examine the machine very closely. Only if I see that it is inoperative because of neglect — for example, a half-century of solitary confinement in a hot, dirty attic — do I give full rein to my cardiac enthusiasms. In this situation, though much work may need to be done, one is justified in feeling that it can be done. With investment of the proper quantities of time and effort, of thought and concentration, the box will one day sing as it did the day it left its maker's hands. However, if I see evidence that someone else has already worked on the box, then the yellow flag of caution comes up fast and hard. The putterings and tinkerings of an unknowledgeable restorer can do irretrievable harm, effectively putting the box beyond any hope whatever of eventual salvage. When I behold the sign of the Hand of the Hacker, more than my antennae start to quiver.

In music-box circles, the term hacker is one of supreme opprobrium. It's not at all like in computers. A music-box hacker is an undiscerning, uninformed, unqualified blockhead who rushes in with his hammer, pliers, and screwdriver where experts would spend months just studying the situation. By the time the expert is ready to begin his hands-on work, the hacker has long since finished, leaving the machine with unsightly and improperly replaced parts; all manner of dents, bumps, and gouges; holes where no hole should exist; great, unsightly heaps of solder; and components misaligned such that the music sounds as if it had been composed by John Cage, rather than Verdi. And to literally add insult to injury, the hacker will show his work with great pride to anyone he can maneuver close enough to the scene of the crime. "Ain't that something?" he'll beam at his dubious, or even frankly horrified, audience. "Didn't play a note before, and now just listen to it!"

The Kingdom of Hackerdom draws its citizens from many principalities. There are clockmakers and watch restorers; there are jewelers. Some machinists are music-box hackers. So are public-school shop teachers. Many household Mr. Fixits hack at music boxes. In point of fact, the great majority of these destructive legions are highly capable workers in their fields, but they seem to share a peculiar lack of appreciation for the extraordinary individuality of form, assembly (and consequently voice) of fine antique music boxes. Miss a subtle clue along the way, such that you alter a particular setting by as little as one or two thousandths of an inch, and you'll silence the soul of the maker, perhaps forever.

Mention music-box hackers to a master restorer, and you're likely to bring him to the edge of apoplexy. A lifetime of working at undoing hacker damage has persuaded most of these professional artists that by comparison, Sisyphus had a sinecure. When Nancy Fratti decided to open her Restoration Academy for Hopeful Hobbyists, she had to contend with the outraged splutterings of that greatest master of them all, the late Elton Norwood. Elton insisted that her educational venture would cast her as nothing less than an accomplice before the fact in a crime –- and a major crime at that. Isn't a little bit of knowledge dangerous? Well, then! Didn't Nancy see that she would be turning loose hordes of minimally-trained amateurs to gleefully and eagerly fall upon fine music boxes like locusts on a cornfield. Elton insisted that only experts should work on these machines.

Nancy supported her position with a number of arguments, but

I think the most cogent was her belief that if anything, attendance at her school would have the opposite effect. "Someone who's got more enthusiasm than brains is just plain going to hack at music boxes," she told Elton. "He doesn't need any help from me. But maybe, if he comes to a school like this, he'll at least learn that it ain't so easy as it looks. The students who can get really good will see what that's going to take on their part. And the others might just learn what their limits are. Which does not mean, by the way, that they can't have a hell of a lot of fun doing what they *can* do, and doing it well."

I've got to go with Nancy on this one. As a very obvious member of the second group, I've derived more satisfaction and pleasure from music boxes than I'd ever have dreamed possible, while staying strictly within the bounds of my competence. Moreover, I've had the pleasure and satisfaction of watching those boundaries expand as the result of continued practice and study. In addition, I've been impressed by the manner in which Nancy and her associate, Joe Roesch, have been able to help skilled machinists, clockmakers, and hobbyists to adapt their considerable technical skills to music box work.

I've often wished there were some sort of Hacker Police, a group perhaps along the lines of the Drug Enforcement Agency, whose job it would be to swoop down on music box hackers, and bring them to justice. Part of the sentence would be mandatory corrective time to be spent at Fratti Academy. Should such a police force ever come to exist, I will be first in line to inform. I even have a target in mind, a fellow by the name of Willy Harding. Talk about clear and present dangers!

Willy Harding is one of those fringe figures in music-box collecting circles. He pays no Society dues, comes to no meetings, and shows not a shred of genuine interest in music machines. That's because he has none. In point of fact, Willy is a hoarder. He's a pack rat. A bachelor, he lives alone in a seven-room house in Seattle which could easily contain a family of four. Willy himself occupies two rooms: a bedroom and the kitchen. And since he keeps a few chairs and a little table more or less accessible in what ought to be the living room, I guess we could give him credit for another half-room. The rest of the premises are filled with stuff. Yes, *filled* with *stuff*. Filled, because the piles go clear to the ceilings, leaving only the most narrow of meandering trails through which an intrepid explorer might wander to eyeball the troves. And stuff, because there is neither limitation as to what Willy will accept for long-term storage, nor the slightest semblance of order in his amazing repository.

Willy's prominent eyes and perpetually open mouth give him the look of an eager fool. But it's not a good idea to underestimate him. As is often the case with extremely eccentric people who have managed to survive to middle age or beyond, Willy is long on shrewdness. Stories abound regarding highly-esteemed collectors who set out to do a little horse trading with that moronic junk yard proprietor, and ended up losing their shirts right along with their prize mares.

In point of fact, although Willy's house is cluttered in the extreme, it definitely is not a junk yard. Willy isn't quite your typical pack rat. The building blocks of his treasure mounds are Tiffany lamps, and Sèvres porcelain, and eighteenth-century brass microscopes, and nineteenth-century first editions, and fine Vienna bronze statues. And — since they *are* highly valuable items these days — music boxes. Willy definitely goes for the good stuff. When I think of what-all is piled up at Willy's place, unprotected by either burglar alarm system or sprinkler device, I can bring myself close to a panic attack.

Who is this Willy, and how and where does he come by all this stuff? I wish I could tell you. All anyone seems to know is that some twenty years ago, he took off from his family's farm in Iowa and landed in Seattle. "My father and my grandfather before him, they spent more'n fifty years sloppin' hogs at five o'clock in the morning," he once told me. "And I figured that that was a bad habit to get into. So I left while the leavin' was still good." What Willy has done for income in place of hog-farming, though, is anyone's guess. Ask him what he does, and he'll answer, "I'm in business." Ask him what kind of business, though, and he'll tell you that you need not be concerned: he attends to his business, just like maybe you should attend to your own.

Neither is there any solid clue as to the origin of Willy's

amazing volume of treasure. But here, I can make a fair guess. Though Willy does spend a lot of time poking through flea markets and estate sales, that couldn't begin to account for the stuff he's got piled up in his house. My bet is that Willy has a really spectacular network of pickers.

Pickers are an interesting lot. In a manner of speaking, they form the basis of the food chain in antiques and collectibles. They know their territories, and they scour the land endlessly, looking to uncover that one super piece that will make the entire day worthwhile. They roam through the flea markets and the good shows; they visit junk yards. And they knock at your front door. "Got any old stuff you might want to sell?" they ask. Or, they may say that they're collecting newspapers. The object is to get into your house, where they can take a look at what's there. Not that they'd steal it — in conventional terms, most pickers are scrupulously honest. What they *will* do, though, is talk you out of your salable items. The best pickers have an eye for value that's nigh-on supernatural, and a knowledge of the market to match. "I like that little teapot," the picker will tell you. "It's kinda cute. I could give you ten bucks for it." Then, he'll sell the eighteenth-century Whieldon pot to a dealer for two hundred dollars. The dealer, in turn, will put it on his shelf at twelve hundred, which leaves him room to discount it to a thousand for his faithful collector-customers.

Pickers make their living on volume: they need quick, reliable turnover, and they definitely prefer cash, and no receipt, thank you. Word travels rapidly through picker networks about guys like Willy. "He'll take anything, long as it's decent stuff." "He's a good joe; he don't try and jew a guy down; just pays your price." I suspect that the parade of pickers to Chez Willy is an everyday event, and that most of the time, it goes on well into the night.

Certainly, a Willy can be helpful, even useful, to a collector. It's impossible, of course, to enjoy his collection — he doesn't *have* a collection, as such — but if you happen to be looking for a particular machine, or a part, let's say, then Willy's is a reasonable place to start. Because the odds are pretty good that somewhere in his house, he'll have what you're looking for. And given that his costs of acquisition were probably quite low, he can sell it to you at a very fair price and still make himself a profit. You just have to be willing to set aside a day to paw through his house with him, and not mind a few cuts and bruises from the inevitable occasional avalanche. But if you're not willing, you're really not much of a collector, are you?

My story of Willy, the Mad Hacker begins on the day I called him to ask whether he might just have a spare comb for a Regina disc music box that I was working on. He paused for just a moment to consult his intracerebral filing system. "Oh, yeah," he said. "Sure. A Regina comb? You bet. I got a big box, all full of extry combs, and I'm positive there's a Regina one in there. 'Course, I don't know exactly where the box *is*, and you're gonna have to . . ."

"I know, Willy," I said. "I'll have to come over and help you look for it. That's fine; I'll enjoy the hunting. Saturday be okay?"

"If it's Saturday, it's gotta be after lunch," Willy said. "By the time I finish the Everett Flea Market, and then drive all the way down to Midway for *that* one, and then get back to Seattle, it's usually after one o'clock."

"Fine, Willy," I said. "I'll see you about two."

Willy was waiting when I got there; he had a can of beer in his hand, and he took me straight through to the refrigerator, where he gave me a can. I took it gladly. It was going to be a long afternoon; long and warm. Long and warm, with much dust in the throat.

By the end of two hours, we'd gone through perhaps a quarter of the material in the living room, and most of the stuff in each of two children's' bedrooms. Not in any sort of orderly fashion, however. We'd root away at one pile or another for a while, and then, suddenly, Willy would have an inspiration, and lead us into another region, or even into another room altogether. Just what odd sorts of connections were striking sparks in his head, I couldn't say. Maybe he'd come upon a piece whose arrival had been contemporaneous with the sought-after box of combs. Or he might have noticed an item in whose company the combs had been seen at one time or another. Who knows? As far as I was concerned, the needle was as likely to be in any one haystack as any other. I followed Willy's whims without annoyance or complaint. Finally, he stood up and scratched at the top of his head. "Hey, I bet I know," he announced. "I bet I put them down in my workshop."

I suspect that at that point, I gave him a pretty peculiar look. "You have a *workshop* here, Willy?" I said, and in the privacy of my own thoughts I added, Under *what*? I'd have been no less surprised if he'd told me he had a formal library and solarium tucked away someplace.

"Oh, sure," Willy said. "Y' gotta have a place to work on things, don't you? It's down in the cellar; come on."

He led me through the kitchen and down a flight of narrow, circular wooden steps, where despite his low overhead warning, I nonetheless managed to crack my noggin against a projecting beam. I was still rubbing the sore spot when we hit bottom. Willy fumbled for a moment, and then pulled a light cord.

The sight staggered me. Willy's basement stretched the full extent of the house above, and every available inch, it seemed, was as full as the rooms upstairs. But these were the big things. On one side of the room, phonographs were piled — that's right, piled one on top of the other — three-high. Giant wardrobes, salvaged, perhaps, from some Brobdingnagian palace, stood shoulder to shoulder with comparably-massive chests of drawers. A far corner seemed to be full of statues, stone, bronze and plaster all mixed together, some as much as eight feet in height. And to my right was a neat pile of what I at first thought were disc music boxes, but then I realized they were oblong, rather than square, and wider at one end than the other. They were children's' coffins. Immediately, I looked away; I didn't want Willy to intercept my stare, and possibly open one of them up. If there was anything inside, I didn't want to know about it –- let alone know what that anything might be. "My God, Willy," I said. "I never knew you had all this stuff down in a basement."

Willy laughed, and dismissed my amazement with a wave of his hand. "This isn't everything," he said. "I got five storage lockers, too. And every one of them's as full as this house." As I stared at him, he added, "Five *big* storage lockers. Biggest size they rent, in fact."

"So, what you're telling me is that your box of combs is someplace in Seattle," I said. "You've got it narrowed down that far."

"Nah, nah." Willy laughed again. "They're here; I'm sure about that. Come on — we'll go look over by the workbench."

I followed him past the coffins and around a corner of deco

floor lamps. From here, we set off along a winding path through the piled oak, marble, and mahogany treasures, just barely wide enough for one person to go sideways, assuming he was careful. It was a journey I'd never have attempted without an experienced guide. At last, we emerged into a clearing, at the far side of which I could see, amazingly enough, a large wooden worktable, built in against the wall. On a piece of pegboard behind and above it hung an assortment of tools, and at the back of the table itself were a couple of toolboxes. The tabletop was littered with loose hardware and scattered tools, Roughly at mid-mess sat a container of some sort. As I came up close, I saw that it was a small, narrow, rectangular box of unadorned walnut, and that it had three thin brass bars protruding from its left side-panel. Heart against breastbone —- thud! It was a music box.

Not just a music box, either. This was a very early cylinder box; the fact that the controls actually emerged from the contours of the box proper, rather than being confined behind a hinged wooden flap suggested a manufacture date prior to 1840. I had every reason to expect that the music on this box would be outstanding. Quite likely, exquisite arrangements of four operatic selections. All at once, a comb for a Regina was the farthest thing from my mind.

"That looks like a nice music box," I said.

Willy was probably sorting through his intracranial connections, to see whether he might find a lead to the box of combs, because he just blinked at me for a moment before he followed my pointing finger with his eyes. "Oh, yeah, yeah . . . I guess so," he said. "That was one I *had* to buy. This guy who owned it, he also had a big Fereiras box, one with a whole load of interchangeable barrels, you know? Well, I wanted the Fereiras box, but he wouldn't sell it to me unless I took this one, too. So, what the heck, I figured. Why not?"

The first time I ever heard a person refer to a Fereiras box, I was more than a little taken aback, but I soon came to understand. The Swiss companies Nicole Frères and Mermod Frères, who made many good-quality music boxes during the nineteenth century, are nowadays frequently transliterated as Nicholas and Murrmahd Fereiras, respectively — in either case, often shortened to just Fereiras. *Sic transit gloria*, indeed.

Right at that moment, though, I couldn't have cared less about which branch of the Fereiras family had produced the object of Willy's desire. I was fully focused on the machine in front of me. Willy did just say he hadn't wanted to buy it, didn't he?

"It doesn't work, though," Willy said. "The thing won't even run."

First, he didn't want to buy it, and now, it won't even run. "Well, fine," I said. "Why don't you let me take a look at it? Maybe you'd like to sell it to me. It's a nice cylinder box, and I think I'd enjoy fixing it up."

Willy made a face. "Oh, I don't know," he said. "I kinda thought I might work on it myself. That's why it's out on the table here."

That remark set off a general-alarm brain snit. Though I'd said to Willy that I would enjoy working on the box, I knew that the odds were pretty good that I'd have to send out at least some of the work to a full-time restorer-professional. The earlier the music box, the more exacting were the construction specifications, and the more difficult it is to bring the machine back into proper working order. *And* the more likely is the possibility of inadvertently causing damage. Above all, the amateur needs to know and respect his limits. I was quite sure that Willy had never repaired a music box in his life. Would he even know he had limits?

While I was thinking, Willy lifted the lid of the case. "Sure, you can look at it, though," he said. "Matter of fact, I'd even appreciate it. You do work on music boxes; maybe you could give me a few pointers. Help me out a little, y' know?"

The direction in which I wanted to point Willy and out of what I'd have liked to help him, I leave to your imagination. I tried to convince myself that he was just kidding me along, but to my knowledge, no one had ever accused Willy of owning even a rudimentary sense of humor. I was telling myself a big lie, and I knew it. My only hope was that Willy's routine might represent a shrewd sales ploy — that he was simply trying to get the best possible price for his music box out of me.

This thought was comforting. Because it would be just like Willy. He may not have known the first thing about fine old cylinder music boxes, but he knew I liked them, and would pay a decent price for a nice one. It even occurred to me that Willy might have left that box on the table specifically for me to see, knowing full well that I'd buy it on sight. And if so, he was right.

I could see immediately that the box was a very special one, though it had suffered considerable abuse. The comb and cylinder were some ten inches long, and in that ten-inch spread were packed some 200 comb teeth, thin as needles, and with virtually no space between them. Except, that is, where five of the teeth had been broken out. The cylinder was a fat one — more than three inches in diameter, I was sure — and absolutely studded with pins. Or, to be more accurate, studded with pin holes. Most of the pins had been broken off; the cylinder would need to be repinned. And a glance at the tune change mechanism at the right end of the cylinder told me that the box played not four but three selections.

This was wonderful. Although the casual music box purchaser, trying to get "the most music box for his money," buys a machine that plays as many tunes as possible, the collector approaches the situation from the other direction. With a given number of pins and of teeth, the complexity and artistry of the musical arrangements is inversely proportional to the number of tunes. A late nineteenth century cylinder with ten or twelve tunes can barely manage to fit in even the banal melody lines of its contemporaneous music-hall ditties, but a three-tune box, absolutely crammed with comb teeth and cylinder pins, will play the most gorgeous renditions of selected passages from operatic overtures. In fact, three-tune boxes were not made much after the 1830s, probably because of the degree to which they tested the skills of the music arranger/maker. The time involved in their manufacture must have made it difficult to continue to justify their manufacture. These boxes were in every respect labors of love, the makers toiling months, perhaps years, over them, never being satisfied until the sound of the machine came as close as he could possibly make it to the music he heard in his mind.

Which in turn says a good deal regarding the demands that this particular box was going to put on its restorer. Very small differences would exert very great effects, and I'm speaking of sound qualities as well as appearance. Set the comb a thousandth of an inch too close to the cylinder, or too far away, and the volume of the music would be unpleasantly loud or unacceptably soft, respectively. Set the comb, with those needle-thin teeth, an unmeasurably-small distance off to one side or the other, and the music would instantly lose its ringing clarity, becoming muddled and squeaky, as the pins struck the teeth off-center. And the cylinder pins! Use too hard a grade of steel for the replacements, and the music would be harsh and grating. Place the pins at an incorrect angle relative to the teeth, and the same thing would happen. Use a replacement pin too thick — these pins, I estimated, were roughly ten thousandths of an inch in diameter — and they'd pluck adjacent comb teeth in addition to their proper targets.

All together, then, this was a job for an expert. Were I to try to do this sort of work on this kind of music box, I would be uncomfortably likely to cause irremediable damage to the machine. No, I'd have to send this box to one of the real pros — to David Wells, in Denver; or Dave Beck, in Atlanta; or Christian Eric, in Southern California; or Jim Weir, in Scotland. These were people who not only had been there before, but who lived there, spending day after day, and all day long, in the rarefied atmosphere of the finest old cylinder music boxes. No doubt, I'd lose something by not being involved first-hand in the effort —but that simply could not be helped. A close second-hand would have to do. Perhaps I might be able to go down to the shop for a week or so during the critical comb-cylinder settings. Whoever this particular maker may have been — and I could see no identifying marks — I wanted to be present at the moment that his voice could first be discerned, muffled as it would be by the dense cloud of time. I wanted to be there as the voice worked its slow way forward, aided by the patient, careful guidance of the master restorer. I wanted to be there when at last the voice burst through into full light, releasing upon its audience the full range of the music arranger's passions.

I wiped my forearm across my forehead, and blotted the sweat out of my eyes with my sleeve. I blinked up at Willy, who was grinning at me. "Okay, Willy," I said. "How much do you want for it?"

"Oh . . . no, no." Willy sounded genuinely surprised. "I told you. I don't want to sell it. I think I'm gonna fix it up myself. I oughta be able to handle it; it's not a big one. Be interesting to try."

"But, Willy, look," I said. "Look at that cylinder. It needs repinning. There aren't ten people in the world who repin cylinders. And this box —"

Willy cut me off with a shake of his head and a wave of his hand. *Dis*-missed! "Nah, nah. People make too much fuss over things. You know what *I* think? *I* think people figure that the harder they make something seem, the smarter everybody else'll think they are. Heck, I don't see what's so much about puttin' in some new pins. I got a lathe. What's the big deal?"

"Well, for starters," I said. "What kind of steel are you going to use for your pins?"

He looked at me with that unique blend of pity and annoyance that people usually reserve for the mentally disabled. "What *kind* of steel?" he said. "I don't know. Steel, what difference does it make? I'll go out and buy some steel. What're you driving at?"

I decided to not pursue that line further. Not only useless; potentially harmful. Start talking to him about the intricacies of voicing, and he'd think I was putting him on. Or even making fun of him. Instead, I pointed at the comb. "Those teeth won't be any fun to replace," I said.

Willy's annoyance became more obvious. "What do you think?" he demanded. "I don't know how to use a soldering iron?"

"How about tuning the new teeth?" I said.

"Ah . . . no problem," Willy said. "I talked to a guy about that. All these old music boxes, the comb goes out of tune after so many years. He's gonna lend me his electronic tuner, and then I can bring the *whole* comb in right. Never mind about just the new teeth."

I thought about screaming; if I did, might I wake up? This was getting uglier by the moment. Unless they are rusty, and have therefore lost a proportion of their metallic substance, music box combs NEVER go "out of tune". People sometimes think they do because the expert ears of the makers tuned them to the standards of the time, which usually included a reference-A set to a wave frequency considerably lower than 440 cycles per second. In addition, some of these combs were tuned to meantone scales, rather than according to today's equal temperament. Thus, at first listening, a note here and there may sound "sour" to our ears, but with continued exposure, one becomes acclimatized, and actually pleased, at the novel (and now effective) sound qualities. In any event, trying to retune a comb to modern tuning standards will destroy the proper, designed relationships between the notes represented by different teeth, and therefore will destroy the music as well. And once altered, these changes are not reversible. Where do you go back to? The reference points were left behind, abandoned by the side of the tracks many years ago.

"The governor don't want to run, either," Willy added. "I figure I can rebuild it okay, though. — There's no big trick to that, either. In fact, maybe all it needs is a stronger spring. These old springs can get pretty weak, y' know."

I couldn't decide how to go about this. Here was a magnificent music box, a unique work of art, in imminent danger of being irreparably destroyed. And all at the whim of this moronic, twinkled-toed democrat, skipping blithely from equal opportunity to comparable competence. Why, he was as good as any so-called professional restorer — better, maybe, because he didn't make a big, holy fuss about the work. He just went out and did it!

Still, I didn't want to risk putting Willy down to the point where he'd get sufficiently annoyed that he might discontinue any further negotiations. For the moment, I decided to let things ride. I told Willy to call me if he were to change his mind about selling the music box. He answered sure, sure, and then we resumed our search for the Regina comb.

Willy found the box in fairly short order; it was on a shelf underneath the right portion of the workbench.

"Told you I knew it was down here," Willy crowed.

Somehow, my enthusiasm was less than full-hearted, but I thanked him, forked over the three hundred dollars he asked me for, and went home.

For a week, I stewed and muttered about the endangered cylinder box. "For God's sake," my wife finally told me. "If it matters that much to you, give him a call. In case you didn't know, you can come on pretty strong when you get yourself worked up. But maybe now that he's had a chance to think about it a little, he'd be more willing to sell. Call him; just be casual about it. What can you lose?"

Only a little time, as it turned out. Willy was glad to hear that the Regina comb had worked out well for me, but no, he still didn't want to sell the cylinder box. He was going to fix it up himself.

I waited another week, and then called Willy again.

"Listen," I told him. "This is exactly the kind of music box I really like. It would mean a lot to me to get it working, and then be able to hear it. Why *don't* you sell it me — or trade it, if I've got something you'd like to have instead. If you really do want to work on it, you could work on it with me."

I wasn't going to take a chance of really riling Willy up by saying anything about professional restorers; I thought that once I had sent out the box, I'd invite him to go down with me to watch the critical points in the work being done. Hell, I'd even pay his fare, if necessary. It might be a good investment: maybe he'd learn something in the process. But my idea turned out to be, as they say, academic. By George, Willy just was *not* going to sell me that music box, because it was gonna be *he* who was gonna fix it up. "Maybe I'll sell it to you then," he said. "Fixed up, I can get a better price, right?"

"I'll pay you a fixed-up price for it as-is," I howled. "How much do you want?"

Willy just laughed amiably, and hung up the phone.

As I slammed down the receiver, Myra gave me the fish eye. "Why don't you go mow the lawn," she said. "Or pull some weeds. Chop wood. At least, go outside. I don't want to have to deal with tooth marks on my table legs."

"Very funny," I muttered.

"But there's nothing you can do about it," she said. "It's his music box — and if he doesn't want to sell it, there's no way you can get it."

"That's what's so frustrating," I said. "He hasn't done anything illegal. There're no authorities I can complain to. There really *is* nothing I can do. He's got sole power to simply destroy something of real importance, and nobody in the world can lift a finger to stop him."

"That's the problem," said Myra. "That music box is very important to you, but it's not to him."

"Tell me," I said. "He comes over here and listens to my cylinder boxes, and then says he doesn't know why I make such a fuss over them. He says he has absolutely no idea what it is I hear in them."

"Well, there you are," Myra said. "Go tell a man who's been blind all his life to appreciate a sunset."

I'm not sure I've ever felt more helpless and lonely. I flopped into my armchair; might as well have a good sulk. But after a moment, I sat up and cast a tentative verbal net into my surging tide of uncertainty. "Hmmm," I said. "Y'know what?"

Myra lowered her knitting and stared at me, her acknowledgement at least as tentative as my foray.

"I'm thinking," I said. "And it occurs to me that Willy may just be playing with me. So far as I know, maybe he did plant that box for me to see and get hooked on. And he is a pretty shrewd guy --- maybe he picked up on just how hooked I was."

"Which wouldn't have taken terribly much perceptiveness," said Myra.

No point trying to argue that one. "He's not greedy, either," I went on. "Whatever else he is — and he's plenty —he isn't greedy. But he does like to play the game. He must know what he wants for that music box. So, I think I just have to be patient, and eventually, it'll come my way. But the more I go after him, the more fun he has. And as long as I keep playing, he will."

Myra shrugged. "Could be," she allowed.

"I think so," I said. "Actually, the more I think about it, the more I think I'm right. People who fix things usually talk about it; they like to show off their work. But I've never known Willy to fix a thing. No one has. I really do think he's just playing.

I can't say I forgot about Willy's music box, but I was able to stuff it into one of those rear-mind pigeonholes that are reserved for those troublesome ideas and notions which, given free rein, would bring our lives to a grinding stop. Every now and again, the machine would remind me of its presence, by grabbing onto some visual or verbal connection in my everyday life, or by squirming its way into a dream. So, several months later, when Willy called to ask me to come by and "talk about that music box," I was instantly ready. In fact, I was almost as instantly over there.

Willy greeted me at the door, and led me along the narrow trail through the *terra incognita* of the living room. "I've been thinking about it, and I figure you really oughta have that little music box," he said. "Any way you cut it, that kind just doesn't do much for me. I'd rather listen to one of those neat boxes with the drums and the bells — gives the music a little pizzazz, y' know?"

"Sure, Willy," I said. "Sure. That's great."

Sure, I knew. *De gustibus non est disputandum,* and I had no intention of disputing this particular expression of taste in any way. Why should I? Let Willy have his bell boxes; why not? As long as he was willing to let me have what I appreciated. I was just grateful that I'd been right. He'd had his fun; okay, then. Now, the game was over. It was time to sell.

We went down the cellar steps, hung a hairpin right at the coffins, and walked up to the workbench. The box was still there, right at the center of the table, exactly where it had stood the last time I'd been down there. Thank God!

"Well, there she is," Willy said.

At that moment, I noticed that the lid was open. On the last visit, it had been closed. I rushed forward, and peered down into the box.

I gripped the edge of the table with hands suddenly gone icy and wet; otherwise, I'd have certainly either grabbed Willy by the neck, or toppled to the floor. Willy, however, didn't seem to notice my distress. Either that, or he mistook it for uncontrollable ecstasy. From my left, he reached forward. "Here," he said. "Lemme play it for you."

If it were possible, I'd have stopped him, but all I could do was hang onto the table while my enemy impaled me on the second prong of his horrible weapon. My first impression upon looking down into the case was that of being exposed to the results of a particularly gruesome ax-murder, but now, as the cylinder began to turn, I realized that that would have been a bargain. In fact, I was looking at the victim of a maniac even more hideously deranged than a mad hatchet-wielder. This machine had once been a prima vocalist, a performer of the finest music ever created, with a voice as glorious and thrilling as they came. With toil, with pain, and above all, with love, her maker had created music particularly suited to her outstanding vocal capabilities, and had spared nothing in time or effort to assure that she would perform it flawlessly. Now, she had been subjected to the most brutal attack imaginable, and left with both ghastly disfigurations and dreadful brain damage. Once, this music box had thrilled audiences on at least two continents with her renditions of selections from *Trovatore*, or *Gazza Ladra*, or *Robert le Diable*. Now, she sounded like a disabled preschooler, trying (with marginal success) to manage *It's Howdy Doody Time*.

The entire machine was an outrage. The garbled nature of the music probably was due to two factors: for one thing, Willy had clumsily replaced the cylinder pins with new steel of far too great a diameter, so that with the closely-packed teeth of the comb, the pins were as likely to produce a wrong note as the correct one. For another, the little steel peg to the right of the cylinder, the adjustment of which registers the cylinder — that is, it aligns the cylinder, with its rows of pins, in proper relationship to the teeth of the comb — was missing, having been replaced with a small nail that Willy had soldered into place. He must have broken off the original; then, whether he'd given any thought to the correct length of the replacement, or simply soldered it in, Willy-Nilly, I couldn't say. Whichever, the so-called tune was unrecognizable as music. It was simply a random-sounding assortment of horribly loud, twanging notes (because the replacement cylinder pins were too long, too heavy, and improperly angled with respect to the teeth; and the comb was placed too close to the cylinder), interspersed with the a generous assortment of squeaks, groans, and burp-like noises, the result of either absence or poor placement of the damper wires which should mediate the interaction between pin and tooth.

The spring barrel was dented: Willy must have squeezed it between the jaws of a giant vise to do God-knows-what to the spring. He must have gone after the governor with a mallet: it was covered with scratches, scrapes, and odd, semilunar peen marks, and it ran with an irregularly-irregular rhythm, which lent to the music some tempo dynamics hitherto unheard, let alone even considered, in all music's annals. The comb was a welter of scratches, whether due to an idiotic attempt to "tune" teeth, or mere carelessness, I have no idea. The five replaced teeth were monsters of deformity: thick, crooked, and shaped utterly out of proportion to their neighbors. The solder that held them in place was heaped in gray mounds that suggested the comb had been subjected to aerial attack by squadrons of terrorist pigeons. And then — *then* — as the performance came to a merciful close, Willy added a literal insult to his injuries by leaning past me to close the lid of the case. The central portion of the lid had been gouged out, to permit the hacker to insert a small oval wooden inlay, a pan-pipe and a horn at diagonals, straight off the shelf of one of the local hobby shops. "Those plain lids are awful dull," I heard the assassin say. "Thought I'd give it a little pizzazz."

Lest I be accused of hyperbole, I want to say that in this case I definitely consider assassin to be a term of understatement. For close to two hundred years, that music box had transmitted, and in the most magnificent fashion, the sorrow and the anguish, the joys and the triumphs, of a particular human life. Whoever may have been the person behind that voice, there was something he needed to tell us, something important, something that mattered very much to his listeners, as well as to him. And now that voice was silenced, forever. Through the music box, the maker had lived; now, he was truly and in all respects dead. One might argue that Willy's act was more manslaughter than murder in the first degree, but so what? Either way, the maker was dead. I would never have the opportunity to hear what he so badly wanted me to know. Did I want to cry? Scream? Grab up a hammer from the workbench, and fall upon Willy? All of the above?

"Funny thing." Willy sounded as though he were speaking from a great distance. "I think that I probably wouldn't have ever gotten myself up to fix it, except for how excited you got over it. I kept thinking, I can't figure out just what it is about these things that gives you such a charge. So, I thought I'd fix it up — maybe then I could tell, know what I mean?" He shook his head. "But I gotta say, you still got me. I mean, the thing sounds o-*kay* . . . but it sure ain't nothing special, at least not as far so I can tell. Anyway, what the hell: nothing ventured, nothing gained, right? And it didn't take me all that much time. So now, I'll sell it to you. Does a thousand sound okay, since it's fixed up? I mean, if it ain't just exactly right to your specifications, it shouldn't be at that much work for you to get it the way you want it."

Extremes of bad behavior — whether cruelty, savagery, vindictiveness, stupidity, or insensitivity — tend to have a silencing effect upon an audience. Right then, I couldn't manage to tell Willy that the cruel mutilations he'd inflicted on the machine had put it past anyone's help. It was beyond all the king's horses and all the king's men; it would probably even have caused him who had so readily raised Lazarus to throw up his hands in horror and despair. And it had been I who'd given Willy the encouragement he'd needed to do his evil work. Was ever the term 'unwitting accomplice' so apt? As blind in my own way as Willy was in his, I had provided this cheerful slaughterer with all the encouragement he'd needed to maim and kill.

In a froth of self-accusation, I asked myself what I could have done to prevent the disaster, but I came up blank. The box belonged to Willy; he was free to do with it as he wished. Persuasion would have been a waste of time; threats and demands would have produced only a slammed door. Maybe I should have stolen the box, had it properly restored, and returned it to its owner? No, I thought, no use of that. He'd probably have said that it didn't sound so hot to him, and then set about trying to improve it. After he'd had me arrested, of course. Because I — not he — would have done something unlawful. The notion was enough to drive me past the borders of rational behavior.

I tried to comfort myself with the thought that even if there did exist an authority to deal with crimes of this nature, it would likely have been ineffective in rehabilitating Willy. For punishment to be effective, a person first has to recognize and acknowledge that he has committed a crime. And as to education, no amount of time at Fratti Academy or anywhere else can have the least effect on a mind convinced that all that fancy stuff is no more than window dressing. No, Willy would most assuredly have been a recidivist. If only the treatment for a second offense were amputation of the offender's hands — or at least his thumbs. *That* idea appealed to me.

Digging deep into his store of inspiration, a man once created a singular work of art, a marvelous music box. Nearly two hundred years later, another man (with the help of his unwitting accomplice) wantonly destroyed it. How does one reconcile this? How can we be so good *and* so bad? "Created half to rise and half to fall,"

Alexander Pope said of us, in recognition of our astonishing duality of nature. No less than Willy, we all have — and express — an impressive capacity for thoughtless or mindless evil. Our intentions may be the best, but the universe is simply too big and too diverse; isolated as we are in our individual little worlds, and with all those distressing blind spots in our fields of vision, we cannot even come close to encompassing it all. Without ever realizing what we're doing, we destroy a magnificent music box. Or perhaps a lovely woodland meadow. Or a marvelous opportunity. Or a dear friendship. Or a husband, or a wife, or a child. Or a neighborhood. Or an entire nation. Pope went on to refer to us as "the glory, jest, and riddle of the world." Some jest, Alexander! Who did you hear laughing?

I'd like to tell you that I picked up the poor music box and put it out of its disgrace by smashing it on the concrete cellar floor; I'd like even more to say that I picked up the box and smashed it over Willy's head. But lacking sufficient courage, I suppose, I created neither of those dramatic scenes. I just told Willy that his careless, if well-intentioned work had ruined the box for all time, that therefore, I did not want to buy it, and that I'd be just as happy if he were to scratch my name out of his phone listings. Then, I went home, and spent the rest of the afternoon listening to my music boxes, one after another after the other. That helped — but I still had bad dreams for weeks afterward. They stopped only after I went for a walk one afternoon through a local antiques mall, and happened to come upon a fine key-wound cylinder music box in nonworking condition.

The Story of Honest Abe's Music Box

e claim to love Truth, but we don't, not really. Which is altogether understandable. How could anyone love such a heartless jade, one so uncharitable, so ungenerous, so mercilessly unkind? Her countenance is as ugly as her spirit — look at that tight, thin-lipped mouth, those taut features, the glaring, accusing eyes.

But the lady's been cagey in courting the press. Throughout the ages, the supposed goodness and beauty of Truth have been touted from some very high places indeed. It's understandable, then, that we're forever serenading her by moonlight and dedicating ourselves to her in battle. But that's as far as our devotion ever goes. Let the lady emerge from the shadows, ready to accept our embrace, and we run as if we'd seen the bogeyman. And till the light begins to creep back into the morning sky, we take comfort in the arms of our real and eternal love, Truth's half-sister, the beautiful Story.

Story is gentle; Story is kind. Beneath her flowing white robes, Story's movements are graceful and pleasing. Her hair is soft, and her smile warm. Her soft voice caresses and soothes our senses, and for as long as we are in her loving presence, we are content. From little children to our oldest, dim-eyed centenarian, no one is immune to Story's charm. We court her all our lives long, and the more avid our suit, the more generously she confers her favors on us.

Some people are born knowing this; others have to learn it.

The writer who's certain he has the Great Novel in his clutch —- who thinks that all he has to do is transfer the details from life to paper, just as they happened —- inevitably comes to realize that his *magnum opus* is turning out on paper exactly as it did in the flesh. Any way he cuts it, it's boring. Will you have your tedium rare, well-done, or medium? So, the writer starts to dress it up a little. Ah, that's better! Now, a little more. By the time he's finished, often some years down the road, he has to dig hard and think long to identify the kernel of actual happenstance at the heart of his narrative. And usually, he comes to think of his final recorded effort as the real version. Which, by the way, is to his mind and heart even better than true.

We're all writers, whether we record no more than the accounts of our own lives, and beware the man who goes to unusual lengths to profess and proclaim his truthfulness. Look at Ernest Hemingway. For all that he prostrated himself in print before Truth's altar, even the most cursory examination of his life shows how deeply and hopelessly enamored he was of Story. As another example, consider an acquaintance of mine whose habit it is to preface remarks with the words, "I'll be honest with you." As soon as I hear that, I am on four-alarm alert. For what is about to come out of his mouth is a whopper — a first-class story, and usually one that will advance his own cause at the expense of mine. I'm aware that my acquaintance does not see it quite that way — but that's part of the very point I'm trying to make.

Antiques dealers love Story, too: think about provenance. The dictionary defines that word as the history of the origin and ownership of an antique or a work of art, but there's no reason to believe that Noah Webster could stand the sight of Truth any better than the rest of us. The provenance of a particular object is its story, whether written or oral, as relayed by the dealer who sells it and/or the person who owns it. It is no different, really, from any novel or short work of fiction. And that being the case, outright fraud in regard to provenance is uncommon. The innkeeper who tells you that you are about to spend the night precisely where George Washington once slept usually *does* believe that his guests cohabit across the ages with the father of their country. And never mind that if the Emperor Franz Josef really did own all the music boxes attributed to his possession, his personal collection would have been in excess of any fifty-year production of the entire city of Geneva. The man showing you the Franz Josef Box in his own collection is certain — absolutely positive — that the spring of this particular machine once was wound by royal fingers. And he can tell you precisely why that has to be so.

Provenance represents a form of classical storytelling, where the narrative may be traceable down a line of generations of tellers. It may even be possible to reconstruct the manner in which the story grew and developed as it was passed along. As an example, I can tell you about the time I came upon Abraham Lincoln's favorite music box.

This particular story begins on the morning that an antiques dealer I know called to tell me he had a music box he was sure I'd be interested in. He wouldn't tell me much about it — just that it was a cylinder box, and a *very* special one. I'd have to come in and hear it.

Now, Very Special Cylinder Boxes are the rarest of commodities on the Seattle market — but what real collector would chance missing out on a Twenty-Years' Wonder. I dropped what I was doing, and drove down to my friend's shop.

He had the machine up on a counter in front of his desk, at the rear of the shop. From half-way across the room, I knew I'd wasted a trip. The box was small — which is not necessarily bad — and it bore the insignia of the Mermod Frères company, a manufacturer of good-quality cylinder music boxes during the latter part of the nineteenth century. But Mermod stayed too long with the game, and by the turn of the century, the only way to make money in cylinder music machines was to turn out huge numbers of small garbage boxes. The music box before me was one such.

My friend greeted me with enthusiasm. "This is one you're not going to be able to leave here," he crowed. He reached over the counter top. "Let me play it for you."

It was painful. Beaming as though he were bestowing upon me a direct, personal gift from St. Cecilia, my dealer-friend compelled me to listen to the entire ten-air program, all ho-hum versions of the usual standard tunes. "The Mocking Bird." "The Blue Bells of

Scotland." "The Campbells Are Coming" (Not nearly soon enough for me, I thought). "The Tyrolienne," from *William Tell.* The Soldiers' Chorus," from *Faust* ("My fa-ther murdered a kangaroo; gave me the gris-a-ly feet to chew . . ."). "Si Nostri Monti" from *Il Trovatore.* "The Manon Waltz." "The Beggar Student March." "The Boccaccio Serenade." "The Jolly Brothers Galop." And each air was rendered to a generous accompaniment of squeaks, squawks, and groans from bent cylinder pins and misaligned dampers. I thought it would never end. When it did, though, my friend asked me whether I had music boxes as nice as this one in my collection.

I didn't know quite what to say, and not only because of the dreadfulness of the music. There was in addition the matter of the price tag. For a box such as this, one collector might ask another, oh, say, six or seven hundred dollars. Allowing for the fact that many nonspecialist antiques dealers appear to believe that almost any music box is a unique treasure, an object of incomparable beauty and inestimable worth, I would not have been shocked by a price tag of a thousand, or even twelve hundred dollars. But the tag on the inner lid of this machine read $1700. For not terribly much more than that, I could have bought a very nice early key-wound music box, with lovely arrangements of music from different operatic overtures.

But then, I remembered that the dealer had specified that this was a very special box. Well, okay; there was my opening. I asked him just what was so special about it.

I hadn't thought it would be possible, but my friend smiled even more broadly. "Aah!" he purred. "You can't see it, can you? Fair enough. Well!" By way of compensating for the absence of a drum roll, he cleared his throat. "It just happens to be that *this*..." He gestured at his prize. ". . . was Abraham Lincoln's favorite music box."

This performance set me back more than a little. By both word and action, the dealer had, in the past, convinced me that he was quite honest. Still, I knew that this did not prevent him from consulting with his sweetheart, Miss Story, about the history of his merchandise. Dealers know the depth of their customers' affection for Story, and so, the pretty lady often finds herself involved in transactions of older, well-travelled objects. It's amazing how often a person is induced to buy an expensive antique by a story told by the dealer. And never mind that the dealer may offer a money-back guarantee against misrepresentation. How many people will be inclined later on to send Story packing, in order that they may cuddle up to harsh, ugly Truth?

I was as certain as I could be about my assessment of that box. The music itself indicated a turn-of-the-century origin; in addition, the construction of the mechanism included features not used until the mid to late 1890s. The spring was placed to the right, rather than the left, of the cylinder, adjacent to the governor. At cylinder-left, there was a late-style mechanism for changing and selecting tunes. The winding crank, like that of an early phonograph, was located outside the case and to the right. There was a Jacot Safety Check, a feature to prevent destruction of comb and cylinder in the event the governor were to give way; these were not used until 1886. And if definitive proof were needed, a small nickeled plate to the right of the spring listed several of the Mermod patents used in the construction of the box. Since the latest patent date was 5/8/88, by which date Lincoln had been dead some 23 years, it was difficult for me to accept the dealer's claim at anything like face value. Still, I thought, he didn't just pull that line out of the air. "Tell me," I said to him. "Just how do you know this was Lincoln's favorite music box?"

He didn't bat an eye; his smile didn't weaken for an instant. The guy wasn't lying; what he was about to say, he believed. "The owner of the box told me," he said. "She's got papers that tell all about it. They go with the box; the buyer gets them. They tell all about how the box belonged to Governor Pierce, of Nebraska. He was a friend of Lincoln's, and Lincoln used to come to his house to listen to the music box. The governor lived with his two spinster sisters, and when he died, they inherited the music box. It was purchased from their estate in 1901, and the present owner bought it in 1943."

This was interesting. "Let's see those papers," I said.

"You can't," said the dealer. "Not right now."

I looked at him.

Now, he sighed. "The box is here on consignment," he said. The owner's an older lady — oh, you know. Kind of crotchety. She wouldn't give me the papers. What if they got lost, or dirty, or something? Then, her box wouldn't be worth nearly so much. If somebody wants to buy the box, she says, then they can have the papers."

Now, my friend started to look just a bit nervous. "Quit staring at me like that," he said. "What's the matter — don't you believe me?"

If I had not known the man, I'd have just said that I didn't believe Abe Lincoln had ever heard this music box, let alone loved it, and walked out of the store. But you can't do that to a friend. Especially where a story is involved, one ought to be careful with a friend's feelings. "Yes," I said to him, "I do believe you. That is, I believe you're sincere. But what I know about music boxes tells me that this one just plain could not have been Abe Lincoln's favorite."

"Well," the dealer said, just a little too lightly, I thought. "Why don't you tell me why not."

This was a crossroads situation. Push ahead, and somebody is likely to be hurt. "Do you really want me to?" I asked. Or should we leave it the way it is. You believe this was Lincoln's favorite music box, and I don't. You can sell the box to someone else; I'll thank you for the consideration, and we can both be happy."

"No, no," said the dealer. "That's not good. I appreciate your faith in my word, but if I'm wrong, I want to know it. I have faith in you, too, and I know you know music boxes better than I do. So, go ahead; tell me. No hard feelings. I promise."

The last two sentences were by themselves another story. Imagine having no hard feelings against the bounder who tears you away from the arms of gentle Story and forces you to embrace her thoroughly nasty half-sister. But the rules are clear: at this point, the speaker is to be taken at his word. "Okay," I said. "Since you ask, I'll tell you."

As I finished ticking off the reasons that made me believe Lincoln had never listened to this music box, my friend was showing clear signs of disquiet. He shook his head. "I dunno, I dunno," he said rapidly. "They had all the papers there, all right . . . well, I'll tell you what let's do. I'll give the old couple a call. Tell 'em you're a collector, and you're interested, but you need to actually see the papers yourself before you buy."

I almost said that I really *wasn't* interested, that anything I might see on those papers would not influence me in the direction of buying that mechanical musical atrocity at any price, let alone at the insane number on that sticker. But I asked myself why *I* should be so eager to fling *my* arms around Truth's scrawny, unappealing neck. Wouldn't it be both nicer and more interesting to say yes, and then to invite Story, rather than her graceless sibling, to take a look at those papers with me? "After all," said my friend, the dealer. "I did ask you for your opinion. If you read those papers, and then you can still tell me it's not for real, I want to know. Because if that story isn't true, I'm certainly not going to sell this music box as though it were."

"All men kill the thing they love," wrote Oscar Wilde, but he was wrong. In fact, we rely upon hired assassins. I told my friend, all right, I'd go.

An hour later, I was in the living room of a large house on the side of a hill, with a lovely view down into the heart of the city. In probably another five years, a Yuppie-directed real estate ad would be proclaiming the glories of this Gracious Victorian Home — even though the place actually dated from no earlier than the twenties. It was pretty clear that the elderly couple talking to me were getting ready to meet the Saint, which explained why they had placed their music box, along with a number of their other possessions, in the hands of my antiques-dealer friend.

"It's a real pleasure to meet you," the old lady said, with a huge, toothy smile that stretched her skin over her face like a skull-mask. Her hand in mine felt like a dry stick. "Mr. — told us that you collect music boxes. Do you have a lot?"

"Something over a hundred," I said.

"Oh, *my*, Daddy." She looked at her husband, who beamed at her. "Isn't that wonderful! To have someone with so *many* music boxes be interested in ours." She looked back at me. "We've gotten so much pleasure from it for . . . oh, forty-six years, now. I just never got tired of listening to it. But our children live in California and Chicago, and . . . they're just very . . . well, *modern*. You know."

It sounded more like a statement than a question, but I nodded anyway.

"They're both doing nicely, bless them, and they are both fine children. But they live very differently from the way we do; there aren't many things of ours that they will want. And I simply can't bear the thought of people coming in here after we're gone, those awful estate sale people. They put a price tag on everything, or they have an auction; all kinds of strangers come tramping through the house, and in just a few hours, it's all gone. Everything we've loved for so many years, just gone and scattered. No!" Her voice was clipped and firm. "I simply can't bear that thought. I'd rather sell the things myself, and then take the money, and send the check to the children."

She probably always did want to do things herself anyway, I thought. And even though she'd never out and criticize the way her children were living, this *would* be a good way to let them know what she really thought, wouldn't it? Well, fair enough. I nodded again.

"And this makes it even better," she added. "To meet you, and to know that you will be enjoying that music box as my husband and I did for all those years makes it oh, so much easier. So you see, young man, I'm actually quite grateful to you."

I was not pleased at the subtle, but clear, turn in the conversation. To be interested was one thing, but for her to know I'd be enjoying it was something else altogether. Was she an old lady looking to her much-loved music box for assurance that somebody, if not her own children, would recite the prayer for the dead in her memory? Or was she just a wily old dame slipping me the con? I couldn't tell right then what her story was. But in any event, it was not she who was selling the music box; my friend, the dealer, was doing that. And he'd asked me to look the papers over. So I mentioned how eager I was to see the material about Lincoln.

"Yes, of course. I'll go get it right now." The old man, who, until then, had said no more than hello, shuffled off across the hall into the dining room. In a moment, he returned with an envelope. "Open it up," he said, as he handed it to me. "All the information is right inside."

"I'm sure you'll find it very interesting," added his wife.

For the third time, I nodded. "I'm sure I will," I said.

There were three pages folded neatly into the envelope. The

first was a letter addressed to the lady with whom I was then visiting; it had been written on May 22, 1943, by an antiques dealer in Springfield, Missouri. It read:

> I am happy to send along the music box, as we agreed when you were in my shop on your recent trip.
>
> As I told you, I bought the music box, along with a melodeon, in New England from a lady who had inherited them from a sister of one-time Governor Price of Missouri. She told me the melodeon was very valuable because Lincoln loved to play on it and he also enjoyed the tunes of the music box. I am telling you this just as it was told to me, and I have no doubt it is true.
>
> I know you will enjoy this wonderful music box very much. It should reach you within two weeks.
>
> Thanking you for your patronage, I am
>
> Cordially yours,

Attached to the letter by paper clip was a half-sheet of stationary, on which was written in a firm, feminine hand:

Mrs. ——- told me personally at the time I saw the two items in her shop that after Gov. Price's wife died, they (his two sisters) kept house for him, and then, after the governor himself died, they were left with his personal things. As their fortunes dwindled, they were forced to sell most of their beautiful things - these were the last of their possessions left to be inherited.

I looked up. The old lady was smiling expectantly. "Interesting," I said. "Very interesting." And I thought, Price, not Pierce. And governor of Missouri, not Nebraska.

"Yes," she said. "Oh, I'll tell you. Every time I turned that music box on, I could *see* Lincoln. Just as if he were standing there. You know — with his cloak around his shoulders."

Too bad the box didn't play "Battle Hymn of the Republic," I thought, and that gave me an idea. "The dealer said that Lincoln had enjoyed the tunes," I said. "I wonder if he had a favorite."

The old lady's face got even brighter. "I've *thought* of that," she said. "And I think he probably did. I'll bet it was "The Mocking

Bird." That was a very popular song, and it would have reminded him of that girl he loved when he was young, the one who died. You know: 'The mock-ing bird is sing-ing o'er her grave.' Ann Rutledge, that was her name. I looked it up."

"Read the other pages, too," said the old man. He seemed to be speaking very quickly.

"Yes, do," the lady said. "We did some library research on the Governor. It's *very* interesting."

It wasn't terribly interesting, though, not really. Based on a surprisingly large number of books, journal articles, biographical dictionaries, and even doctoral dissertations, the old couple had compiled a two-page synopsis of the life of Sterling Price (1809-1867), governor of Missouri from 1852 to 1856. Though contemporaneous with Honest Abe, there seemed little in the research to indicate that the two men had had grounds for the kind of friendship which would have included afternoon or evening musicales. Price was a Democrat, and fought on the side of the Confederacy during the Civil War. In addition, he died in Missouri two years after that war, and there was no indication as to how either the spinster sisters or the melodeon and music box subsequently made their way to New England, where an antiques dealer from Missouri found them, schlepped them back to their home state, and promptly shipped them right out again to the opposite coast.

"We enjoyed putting that together," the lady said, as she saw me look up from the paper. "It made the music box seem even more wonderful — if that was possible."

I agreed that such would indeed have been a difficult task.

From behind the curtain to the left of the old lady's chair, I noticed Truth. She was pointing a finger, and her nasty, sneering face was one big smirk.

After a glass of lemonade and a plate of cookies, I started back to the shop. I decided to walk, rather than take the bus. What a mess, I thought. Here's a howdy-doo. There was no way on earth that that music box could have entertained our first martyred President. Nothing I saw in print offset the unpleasant fact that the box had not been manufactured until a good quarter-century or more after Lincoln's death. Even disregarding the matter of the patent dates, this style of music box simply *was not made* until the 1890's. There was no way out of this one. I was just going to have to go back and tell my friend that somebody — whether an antiques dealer or a prior owner —had put together a story which had made this particular music box seem more attractive and valuable, but that anyone at all familiar with the field could easily point out all sorts of holes in the fabric of the tale. And if that meant that my friend had to tell the old couple what I had said, and return the box to them to do with as they saw fit, well, that wasn't my fault. What else could I do?

It was not a pleasant walk back to the shop — not with that cruel, spite-ridden female at my side, bickering, sniping, and name-calling the entire way. More than an hour of ill-tempered mono-logue, as self-righteous and tedious on the one hand as it was deri-sive and cynical on the other. How much more pleasant would have been the company of gracious, gentle Story. The further we walked, the more annoyed I became that I'd left her behind with the old couple. Why *couldn't* I have taken Story back with me to the antiques shop? Why hadn't I left her tedious sister to hide her mis-erable face forever behind those living room curtains? With lovely Mistress Story at his side, a person can manage to live with the end-less cruel harassments of that harridan, Truth. But when Story is gone, Truth is the only game in town, and she gives such a turn to a person's screws that life comes to seem a proposition just not worth all that bother.

As I walked through the door of the shop, my friend, the dealer greeted me with a wave. "Well, what do you think?" he called out.

"Tough to say," I answered. "It's hard to know just what to think. I still can't believe this particular music box is old enough to have been heard by Lincoln, but that old couple sure did believe it was. It'd be interesting to be able to trace it back farther —- to talk to the dealer who sold it to the couple back in '43, and then go back through the previous owners. But that's a pipe dream; they've all got to be dead by now."

"So, there's a reasonable doubt, huh?" My friend looked both hopeful and cautiously triumphant.

I looked behind him. The expression of anticipatory disapproval on Truth's hard-favored pan could have turned my stomach. But in my mind's ear, I heard a melodic voice, its beauty and grace altogether compelling. My mind told it to sing louder. "Let's just say a doubt," I replied.

"Well, then, okay," said my friend. "I know you don't want the music box. But what is it worth, really? Is their price *anywhere* near real?"

"It's fine," I said. "I'll take it, and at their price."

As I pulled my checkbook out of my pocket, I had to fight to keep my face straight. To anyone at all experienced in antiques, my behavior meant only one thing: I was pulling a con. I'd bad-mouthed this beautiful music box to pretend lack of interest, which in turn had permitted me to weasel my way into the house, to check on some particular critical point of uncertainty. Then, having certified that I'd struck pay dirt, I was buying, and quick. The fact that I was not trying to haggle meant that the sticker price was in fact a steal. All of which is strictly according to the rules. The fact that the dealer and I were, if not close friends, at least friendly, was of no consequence. In this business, you are supposed to know your merchandise, and if you don't, then you have no right to complain if you end up selling too low. The dealer had not asked me for an appraisal; he'd offered me a machine for sale, and I had decided to buy it. So, that was that. My friend was too much of a pro to make any sort of direct accusation, but he did narrow his eyes more than a bit, and say, "Pretty impressive change of heart, don't you think?"

I nodded. "Circumstances change, and they can change the way you look at a thing," I said. "And value can be pretty broadly defined."

"Guess I'd better watch you a little closer in the future, shouldn't I?" he said, and then he laughed. We were still friends. This was a game he played for the fun of it, and I had injected more than a trace of spice into the contest for him. We shook hands, I gave him my check, tucked Honest Abe's favorite music box under my arm, and went out the door.

The walk home was about three miles, but it went quickly. Story kept pace with me, entertaining me every step with her light, laughing voice.

That evening, I called upon a long-time, close friend, a man who teaches American History at the University. "I've got a present for you," I said, and pulled out Lincoln's Music Box, a bright red ribbon wrapped around it, the bow at the top.

My friend looked at me in an odd way.

"I know you don't collect these," I said. "But I thought you might like to have this one. It's supposed to be pretty special. Abe Lincoln reportedly enjoyed listening to it." Then, I summarized the contents of the papers for him.

"Sterling Price, huh?" my friend said. "Well, wouldn't that be something. I don't know of any connection between Price and Lincoln, but I'd sure enjoy looking into it. Let's hear what this thing sounds like."

I pulled off the ribbon, wound the lever, and pulled the start lever. My friend listened to the entire ten-tune program; his face was like a little kid's on Christmas morning. "My God," he said. "I've never heard anything *like* that before. Isn't it beautiful!"

I came close to making a mock-gagging sound, but just in time, I caught a glimpse of Truth, simpering in approbation behind my friend. "If you say it's beautiful," I said. "Then, it is. Enjoy it."

He looked troubled. "But I can't take something like this from you," he said. "Not just like that."

"Sure you can," I said. "I want you to have it. Your interest in Lincoln and the governor is a lot greater than mine, so the box has to mean more to you than it ever could to me. You can call it an early Christmas present, if you'd like."

Two days later, my friend and I went back to the 1920s Victorian house to collect the papers. The old couple were thrilled: not only a music box collector, but a history professor, an expert on Abraham Lincoln, was interested in their treasure. The old lady agreed pretty quickly that my friend was even a more suitable owner for it than I. "But I'm so grateful to you for *getting* it to him," she cooed, squeezing one of my hands between the two of hers.

"It worked out well all around," I said.

The lady turned back to my friend. "I'll certainly enjoy knowing what you might come up with in your investigations," she told him.

"I'll let you know," he said.

He did spend a fair amount of time looking into the possible association, but since he was using leisure time, an hour here, an afternoon there, it went slowly. Several months later, I asked him what he'd learned.

Not much, he said. All his trails had dead-ended; there was in fact no defined association or specific social connection between President Lincoln and Governor Price, at least not any that he could discern. Nor had he been able to find any record of Lincoln enjoying visits with anyone having a melodeon and a music box. "But who knows what may come up in the future?" he said. "I'll certainly enjoy keeping my antennae out. Besides . . . he paused for a moment. ". . . in any case, I love listening to the thing. *Such* beautiful music. And I'll tell you: sometimes I can almost *see* Lincoln's expression when he might have been listening to a song like "The Mocking Bird. Because . . . oh, nuts! You know what I mean, don't you?"

"I think so," I said.

In point of fact, I was quite sure I knew. Because right then, I could hear Story singing to him –- just as I could hear her singing to the old couple in the big house, and to my dealer-friend. And to me. How easy it would have been to be careless, and lazy, and thoughtless, and to have condemned us all to listen *ad nauseum* to Truth's sad, pointless, and uninteresting little morality tale. Yes, the affair cost me a little money, but all right. This was a game with no losers, myself included. What's the going price on a kiss from a pretty lady?

Show Me the Way to Go Home

We wander through our lives along strange routes; we prowl endlessly in unfamiliar territory. We're forever scratching at itches we can't quite reach, or stretching out on beds with lumps in precisely the most inconvenient place. How wonderful it would be to feel comfortable, once and for all time! If only we could find our way home.

But Thomas Wolfe has banished us to perpetual exile –- or so, most people would have it. The conventional wisdom lost no time in sucking up the title of Wolfe's book, that it might ever thereafter be spat out as one of those cute little homiletics, so useful for making a final point in a discussion, while at the same time demonstrating the intellectual profundity of the speaker. "Well, but like, y'know . . . you can't go *home* again," I recently heard a young woman in my office say to a co-worker who'd been unfortunate enough to mention that she was considering moving back to the small town in which she had grown up.

Admittedly, finding the homeward track is no easy thing, but it may not be impossible. Maybe it just depends on how you look at the situation.

I spent the first half of my life in New Jersey –- practically in Gustave Brachhausen's back yard. Gustave Brachhausen was the founder of the Regina Music Box Company, but at that time, I had never heard of Gustave Brachhausen or Regina music boxes. It was not until I was firmly settled in Seattle, many years later, that I ever permitted myself to give a serious thought to a music box. Could a childhood ever have been more deprived? Could a youth ever have been more dreadfully misspent? Since the 1989 Annual Convention of the Musical Box Society International was to be held in Teaneck, New Jersey, I decided that it was going to be a special sort of homecoming for me.

"But you *are* home," Myra insisted. "You live in Seattle. You've lived in Seattle for close to twenty years. *Seattle* is home, now."

"No," I said. "I may live in Seattle, and Seattle may be a nice place to live. But home it is not. No place can be 'home now.' New Jersey is home, period."

My spouse rolled her eyes, sighed, and walked away. Go talk to a wall.

We flew into Kennedy Airport on a Monday evening, picked up a rental car, and made straight for midtown Manhattan. Within an hour, we were at the Carnegie Delicatessen, eating corned beef sandwiches that threatened to dislocate our jaws, and cheesecake capable of producing instantaneous coronary occlusion. As we finished, I leaned back in the chair, and remarked that the meal had had an odd effect on me: gone was all the tension of the five-hour flight and the drive into the city. I felt calm, and pleasantly relaxed. Even soothed.

"Comfort food does that," Myra said.

"Comfort food?" I'd never heard the term.

"Yeah. Food you got when you were a child is supposed to have that effect on a person. That's why it's called comfort food."

"Mother's milk on rye," I said. "Did this stuff have the same effect on you?"

Myra narrowed her eyes. "It has nothing to do with 'being home'," she said. "You can eat comfort food anywhere."

I could have asked her when was the last time she'd gotten a decent lox on bagel in Seattle, but I decided not to. I was just too comfortable.

The next morning came gray and drizzly. All day, as we made the rounds of Manhattan's used bookstores and antique shops, I kept a nervous eye to the sky. Fortunately, only a few drops fell, and, after another visit to the Carnegie Comfort Station, we bailed out the car from the parking garage, and headed up the Henry Hudson Parkway to the George Washington Bridge. As we drove past 125th Street, I pointed toward the Palisades, across the river. "Remember when we were kids, we used to be able to take a ferry across here?" I said.

"Sure," Myra replied. "Just like we can still do in Seattle. Across Puget Sound. They're even nicer ferries, and it's a prettier ride."

We were two blocks from the Loew's Glenpointe Hotel in Teaneck when I realized we'd brought an unregistered conventioneer with us — the Pacific Northwest Weather God. Clearly, P.N.W.G. intended to show me exactly what he thought of my slighting attitude, for at that moment, he unzipped the sky, and let out the rain. I say it rained; actually, it poured. It came down in sheets, in buckets, in uncontrolled sluices. The water drummed on the car roof; it beat against the windshield harder and faster than the wipers could clear it. As we pulled up under the overhang in front of the hotel, I saw our friend Ralph Heintz, from California, standing there, looking (though he was fully clothed) as if he'd just stepped out of a bathtub.

"Welcome to Seattle," I muttered.

"Welcome home," said my wife.

Wednesday morning, we got up and dressed quietly, hoping to not disturb P.N.W.G.; then, we headed out through the justly-renowned Jersey heat and humidity to drive down to West Orange. I wanted to tour the Edison Museum. "Now, this weather is more like it," I said.

Myra shot me her most caustic glance, pure visual sodium hydroxide. She'd hated that weather when she lived in New Jersey; she hated it no less now. "If you're trying to make me homesick, you are definitely on the wrong track," she snapped.

Fortunately, the car was air conditioned, and by the time we got to our destination, Myra was feeling considerably better. We went through the laboratories and factory, saw and heard some old phonographs, and then found ourselves with a half a day on our hands. I drove into South Orange — and there was Gruning's, the old ice cream palace, still scooping away these thirty years later. More comfort food: a nice, soothing chocolate malted sundae for lunch, and no dissent from Myra. My wife holds that nostalgia of a gastronomic persuasion is a very differently-colored horse, definitely an acceptable perversion. Even one to be encouraged.

But after lunch, when I headed toward Newark, to drive through Myra's old neighborhood, she demanded to know why. "What do we need to do this for?" Not having a ready answer, I just kept driving. As we went past the house in which she'd grown up, Myra observed how small it looked, and how narrow the street appeared. "Anything else strike you?" I asked.

"Yeah," Myra said. "Our stupidity strikes me. When I think about that attic and cellar full of neat old stuff that we just left there after my parents died, I get a pounding headache."

I headed up through Montclair into Paterson, and drove, street by street, through my old neighborhood. Forty years ago, it was such a noisy place, but now it was dead silent. The only sound was that of our car engine. Very different –- disturbing, actually; something terribly important was missing. I drove back to the highway and back to Teaneck.

Thursday morning came bright and cloudless, and the convention swung into full gear. We spent the morning listening to a discussion of how to properly sniff out, track down, and make off with various types of mechanical music machines. Then, after the presentations, Marv and Dianne Polan rounded us up, along with some other friends, and whisked us off to Long Island — this, so that we might repay their last-year's visit to our home, when the convention had been held in Seattle. The Polans' collection was choice. We saw some rare, very early phonographs, and a fine Regina tabletop disc music box with an original decorative bin to hold the discs. Every machine was in top functional and cosmetic condition. Best of all was the Ampico-B grand piano, a superb machine with an expression mechanism that was truly a thing of wonder. Though the louder passages in piano music customarily set the screws between my ears to vibrating, Marv's and Dianne's piano did no such thing. Crash as it might, every note came through crisp and clear, every chord gorgeous.

"I hope you don't mind," Dianne said, as she began to set the buffet table for dinner. "I decided to be lazy. Instead of cooking, I went out and got kosher deli."

I glanced at Myra. "If you tell her that it's fine; you feel right at home," said my wife's expression. "I'll slug you."

I did. But she didn't.

Friday brought the workshops, technical and historical discussions which comprised the formal educational component of the meeting. Only in terms of being scheduled, though, were these sessions formal: all the speakers were gracious to a fault in being willing to respond to whatever questions the audience had to throw at them. What I learned about tuning a comb, setting pins straight on a cylinder, encouraging a balky governor to run, and identifying tunes would probably have taken me years of solitary poring over books and tinkering. "It's amazing," I told Myra. "A medical scientist would share his wife with a colleague before he'd share his lab secrets. These music-box crazies are just the nicest, most generous people I've ever come across in my life."

"So much for the old folks at home," Myra said.

At five o'clock that evening, we trooped into the Mart, for the scheduled three-hour orgy of buying, selling, and trading. As I moved through the large, treasure-packed ballroom, I was impressed with the manner in which the atmosphere of this particular convention activity seemed to be set by the regional members. No question; this was a New York/New Jersey mart. Lots of top-quality stuff; very busy; very active. The urbane sellers, confident in the merits of their merchandise, smiled at the furious mill of customers who were snatching the stuff out of their hands and off their tables, like *yentes* at one of the old Bargain Basement sales at S. Klein on the Square. My eyes filled with tears of nostalgia as I plunged into the fray. And when the final bell tolled, I had acquired ten marvelous souvenirs: a lovely, very early cylinder music box, an attractive small street barrel organ, two severely bruised ribs, and six mashed toes. Myra commented that I looked as though I'd been mugged in the subway. "May be," I said. "But it was a good fight — a *great* battle, in fact. And . . ." I nodded toward my two purchases, one under each arm. ". . . *I* came away with the watch and the wallet."

After another series of workshops, a trip to the Society's collection of mechanical musical instruments at the Lockwood-Matthews Mansion in Norwalk, Connecticut, and the Concluding Banquet, we said our good-byes and got into the car. But this was the end of only the First Convention. The Second was just beginning.

The Second Convention is unstructured. Since the attendees come from all parts of the United States and Canada, as well as Europe, Japan, and even Australia, many of them plan to stay on for a bit. They rent cars, and drive around the countryside near the convention site, visiting members who live in the area. We had a week of this wandering before us.

We began just north of New York City, paying a call on Frank and Lore Metzger. Frank collects, restores, and sells some of the most exquisite rarities in the world of mechanical music. His specialty is miniatures, including musical snuff boxes, pocket watches, or *necessaires* (small boxes containing sewing implements and toilet articles elegantly fashioned of gold, ivory, and mother-of-pearl). Frank also works on bird boxes, automata, musical clocks, and first-quality, very old mechanical organs. For four hours, interrupted only by a perfect lunch-al-fresco, Frank put his personal store of treasures through their paces for our amazement and delight; then, he was gracious enough to take me through his workshop. This was an experience as deeply humbling as it was fascinating. I slept little that night, and for once, did not have it in me to complain about my insomnia.

The next morning, we headed up to New England. The ride began auspiciously, as Myra sniffed out an antiques shop in New Haven, looted it of its extensive stock of Wedgwood ceramic ware, and then discovered that the restaurant across the street had a lobster special for lunch. No icing on any cake could elevate my wife's spirit to the plane of lobster on Wedgwood.

From there, we drove to northern Connecticut, to visit Marty and Elise Roenigk. Elise had just been installed as President of the M.B.S.I.; she and Marty live in a spacious Victorian house, where they keep a world-class collection of fine cylinder boxes, impressive and rare disc-playing machines, and magnificent mechanical organs, large and small. As if the demonstration of these treasures were not sufficient, we were able to watch as Steve Boeck and Alan Bies, two gentlemen from Houston who've been collecting and restoring together for close to thirty years, despite being only about forty years old, made regulatory adjustments to the mechanism of a 3-disc Symphonion Eroica. Stereophonic sound, circa 1900! As evening approached, we prepared to leave, but Elise stopped us. "Aren't you going to stay the night?" she said.

I looked at Myra. "Well . . . sure," I said. "If we're invited."

"What do you think I just did?" said Elise. "Though I really don't know why you need a special invitation. Well, then, come on — let's go out for some pizza. I'll put you up for the night, but I'll be damned if I'm going to cook."

The next morning, we set out for Whitehall, New York, for a couple of days with my special Music-box Muse, Nancy Fratti. On the way, we made a flying stop in Greenfield, Massachusetts, to pick up our friend, Angelo Rulli. Angelo is the Editor of the M.B.S.I. Journal, and a full-time organ grinder and entertainer of justified repute. "Welcome home," Nancy said, as she hugged us at the gate.

Myra gave me the fish eye. I shrugged. "If the shoe fits . . ." I whispered out of the corner of my mouth.

A pleasant putter around the repair shop, and a fine dinner, and then to bed. Morning wake-up call was a novel experience: Nancy set off her reproducing piano at seven o'clock. To be blasted into consciousness by a crashing performance of the *Warsaw Concerto* was, I had to admit, not altogether unpleasant.

After a day of trooping through antiques stores with Nancy and Angelo, we had another repair-shop putter, discussing thoughts and ideas regarding the restoration of various machines. Then, the next morning, Myra, Angelo, and I drove back to New Jersey, to see Sam and Peggy Morgenstern. Sam is a long-time collector of cylinder boxes, and when he was introduced to me at the First Convention, he was foolhardy enough to suggest that I might like to visit when I was in his area. I immediately told him we would *be* in the area in just a few days.

"How could you just invite yourself like that?" Myra asked me later.

"I didn't," I said. "*He* invited *me*. All I did was make the general into a specific."

Myra looked dubious. It still just didn't seem quite right to her, she allowed.

"It felt like the most natural thing in the world," I said.

The visit got off to an interesting beginning, Sam showing us through the living room and den on the main floor. There were a couple of very nice cylinder boxes, but mostly, the displays were glass, including some unusual and colorful Czechoslovakian lamps. As we completed the circle, Sam shrugged. "Well, I guess that's it," he said.

I shot a side glance at Angelo. What in hell was Sam up to? This was *all*? He owned one of the world's outstanding collections of cylinder music boxes, didn't he? Then, I noticed that Angelo was grinning. He and Sam were old friends, and there was a game being played here that the two of them had played before.

"Eh," Sam grunted. "Well, I *do* have a few more things upstairs. Just little stuff, really. You know: crap. But if you really want to see it, I'll take you up."

"Oh, I guess I might like to take a look," I said. "I'm not in a hurry."

As we came to the top of the stairwell and rounded the corner, I stopped cold. Before me were two rooms, simply crammed with cylinder music boxes. I say crammed; they were stuffed. They were jammed; they were packed; they were shoehorned. The music boxes covered tables in the centers of the rooms and filled bookshelves at the periphery. They occupied floor-to-ceiling cabinets. They were stacked on the floor. I didn't know what to say, let alone where to start.

"Like I said," said Sam. "Just a little crap. What do you want to see?"

"All of them," I said.

He shrugged again. "Go ahead. You know how they work. Play any of them you want."

When a music-box collector gives you free operating run of his machines, you are entitled to feel no little honor. Especially when it comes from a collector of Sam's standing. This is a vote of confidence, the specific acknowledgement of acceptance. I had no idea what I might have said or done to deserve the favor, and I still don't. But I was not inclined to argue. I thanked Sam, and walked over to a giant Nicole Frères fat-cylinder overture box on the central table, and pulled the start lever.

What followed was a three-hour debauch of cylinder box music that left me limp at the end. There were overture boxes; there were hymn boxes. There were mandoline boxes, forte-piano boxes, organ boxes. There were very early machines with chain-and-fusee drives. There were huge interchangeable cylinder boxes, sitting proudly on matching tables, and playing hearty, robust arrangements of opera, popular tunes of the time, and patriotic songs of various nations. There were extraordinarily rare boxes, including one that played Oriental tunes, and another pinned with music entirely in minor keys, a machine whose hauntingly captivating sound I still, to this day, can not get out of my head.

Partway through my self-guided tour, Peggy came upstairs to ask whether we might be interested in dinner. "Not yet," Sam told her, pointing a finger at me. "This nice and gracious man is being generous enough to pretend to enjoy my garbage up here, and he is not to be interrupted."

I began to say that I'd be happy to interrupt long enough for dinner, that I could listen again later, but Sam waved his hand. "First music boxes," he said. "Then food. Take your time."

By the time we finished eating, it was after ten o'clock, and I was getting a bit concerned about where we might find a place to stay for the night. I suppose by then, I should have known better. When Myra asked for directions to a nearby motel, Peggy gave her an odd look. "Why, you're going to stay *here*, aren't you?" she said. "I've got the guest room all ready."

As we pulled our pajamas out of the suitcase, I shook my head. "This is just incredible," I said.

Myra looked up. "What is?"

"*This*," I said. "*All* this. We go driving through New England, New York, New Jersey for close to a week. And everywhere we go, it's the same. People we've just barely gotten to know take us in, feed and entertain us as if we were visiting royalty, and put us up for the night. And everywhere, I feel perfectly comfortable the minute we come through the door. No awkwardness at all. It's hello, how are you and welcome, and come on in and see what we stumbled over in a shop last week. So, in we go, and instantly, we're right at home."

"Fancy that," said my wife.

We were to return to Seattle late the next afternoon. But first, we stopped in Summit, New Jersey, where Steve and Jere Ryder made us welcome, and gave us a demonstration of some outstanding music boxes and automata from both their family's collection and their shop stock. Then, after dropping Angelo at Newark Airport, we drove cross-state to the northern-most seashore resorts, Long Branch, Sea Bright, and Atlantic Highlands. I thought about dashing down to Asbury Park, to see whether the Richard Kadrey Gallery was still on the Boardwalk, still seducing teen-aged boys with cylindrical Swiss sirens. But we didn't have time. Probably just as well, I told myself. After a short walk along the beach in the slanting light of the late-summer late afternoon, we got back into the car and started off toward Kennedy.

And then, a strange and wonderful thing happened. That ride northward on the Garden State Parkway was one that the two of us had made literally hundreds of times during those long-ago years of lust and acne, when gas was fourteen-nine a gallon, and a day at the shore was always the right thing to do. I recognized every curve in the road, every twist and bank. The car could have been on autopilot. All of a sudden, Myra began to remark on the buildings along the side of the road. One after another, the old landmarks piled up, all in the same spots, all amazingly unchanged. "My God!" my wife finally shouted, and then —obviously — without thinking, added, "I feel like I'm *home!*"

Well, of course I said "Ha!" in the most arrogant and insufferable way I could, but I knew that this victory was only a technical one. Geographical correlates really *don't* have anything to do with the idea of home: home can not be located on any map. Home is defined by people, not place. And the folks who peopled my birthplace when I lived there are gone now — scattered throughout the world and beyond. When I stood in New Jersey and called out, I heard only faint and hollow echoes — the sound of my own voice, attenuated by a half-century's grinding and polishing, reverberating through the chambers of an empty seashell.

Young people have always demonstrated a strong desire to get out into the world. They want to travel, to live somewhere else, "at least for a while." In this respect, I certainly was no exception. The conventional wisdom is quick to put this behavior down to so-called adventuresomeness, or even rebelliousness, but I don't think that's right. I'll bet that more often, it's just Opportunity, whispering in our ears, telling us that home isn't necessarily where a person happens to have been born. "Get out there," she urges us. "Go look for your home. *Listen* for it. Pay attention to the signs alongside the track. You'll know when you're there."

But most of us don't look, and don't listen. Finally, road-weary and discouraged, we trudge back to our places of birth, only to be ultimately devastated by the realization that home isn't there, either. All gone. We mourn this last, most cruel loss, without stopping to realize that what you can't do is go *back* home. To find your way home, you need to go forward. The accent in the title of Thomas Wolfe's book should be properly placed on the last word — not on the next-to-last.

So, Myra had been right, but only partly so. New York and New Jersey really *weren't* home — but they probably never had been in the first place. And I'd been right, too: Seattle *is* a lovely place to live, but it's not home. Home is no place in particular. Home is wherever music machines bring together people of a common understanding, people who speak and respond to the lovely, private language of the culture. Just push a PLAY lever, and a person dead more than one hundred years begins to speak to you. He tells you of his dreams, his aspirations, and his fears; he describes what he thinks he may understand, and what confuses him. He pours out to you his feelings, his sentiments, and his emotions, wild or tranquil.

You may spend days, weeks, or even years, working on a fine music box that has suffered neglect or abuse. The labor is frequently difficult, often frustrating, but it's never unpleasant — for you know that in another hundred years, when someone pushes that PLAY lever, it will be *your* voice and *your* feelings, along with those of the maker, that will be heard. You're never satisfied for your work to be just good enough —- you need to say everything you can possibly get across. And to this end, your contemporaries join in the conversation. "Play it with the lid closed, not open; you're losing a lot of the bass." "If you rake the pins, they'll strike the teeth at the proper angle, not perpendicularly; then it won't sound so harsh." "Move the treble part of the comb maybe another thousandth back; that'll balance it."

The discourse is endless. As good as a music box may sound, you can never be certain that you're hearing all that it has to say to you. But this is all right — in fact, it's better than all right. Being at home has nothing to do with perfection. Perfection closes all further activity, leaving the participants no choice but to sit around in perfect, unending boredom. Nothing else to hear. Nothing to say. A person may be unhappy at times, yet know he's at home; he may feel pain, or sadness, or disappointment. But he feels. When you're bored, though, you only itch to move on. You know you're not in the right place. You know you're not even on the right track.

and nonfiction works that were originally brought to the reading public by established United States publishers but have fallen out of print. The economics of traditional publishing methods force tens of thousands of works out of print each year, eventually claiming many, if not most, award-winning and one-time best-selling titles. With improvements in print-on-demand technology, authors and their estates, in cooperation with the Authors Guild, are making some of these works available again to readers in quality paperback editions. Authors Guild Backinprint.com Editions may be found at nearly all online bookstores and are also available from traditional booksellers. For further information or to purchase any Backinprint.com title please visit www.backinprint.com.

Except as noted on their copyright pages, Authors Guild Backinprint.com Editions are presented in their original form. Some authors have chosen to revise or update their works with new information. The Authors Guild is not the editor or publisher of these works and is not responsible for any of the content of these editions.

THE AUTHORS GUILD is the nation's largest society of published book authors. Since 1912 it has been the leading writers' advocate for fair compensation, effective copyright protection, and free expression. Further information is available at www.authorsguild.org.

Please direct inquiries about the Authors Guild and Backinprint.com Editions to the Authors Guild offices in New York City, or e-mail staff@backinprint.com.